The Deposition Handbook

A Guide To Help You
Give A Winning Deposition

Virginia A. Lathan

The Deposition Handbook

A Guide To Help You
Give A
Winning Deposition

Fourth Edition

CurryCo Publications
Chicago, Illinois

CurryCo Publications
9644 S. LaSalle
Chicago, Illinois 60628
Phone: 773/785-7082
WWW.CurryCo.cjb.net
Email: curryco50@hotmail.com

CurryCo books are available at special discounts for bulk purchases for sales promotions, premiums, fund-raising, or educational use.
For details, write to above address

Designed by Virginia A. Lathan

Printed in the United States of America

Library of Congress Catalog No. 2008900612

ISBN: 978-0-9636195-7-0

The information contained in this book is general in nature and is compiled by a layperson. The book is no substitute for an attorney. If you have an attorney's guidance available to you, and it is different from that given herein, follow the attorney's advice.

All proper names used in the text of this book have no connection to, or association with, persons or organizations having the same or similar names.

To Lillian Winesberry and Virginia Wilson, my mother and grandmother, for taking me to the library when I was a child.

And for Armand P. Lathan, Jr., my grounded son, for allowing me to practice on my steno machine instead of playing Nintendo all the time.

Also to my precocious daughter, Angela M. Lathan, for constantly fueling me with thousands of ideas for things to write about.

"It appears to me that in Ethics, as in all other philosophical studies, the difficulties and disagreements, of which history is full, are mainly due to a very simple cause: namely, to attempt to answer questions, without first discovering precisely what question it is which you desire to answer."

~ **George Edward Moore** ~
Principia Ethica **[1903]**

Contents

Contents Cont'd

FOREWORD

By Attorney Dale S. Wilson

W hen I first heard about *The Deposition Hand-book*, it was just an idea in Virginia Lathan's mind. At that time she made a strong argument as to why such a book is needed. I listened—mostly out of courtesy—but never really shared her vision. But now that the book is completed, and I've examined first-hand the information it contains, I find it hard to imagine that a guide of this sort had not been made available for witnesses previously.

Ms. Lathan has done a thorough job of focusing on some very basic concerns with which deposition witnesses are confronted. These are concerns that most attorneys tend to overlook because they themselves are so familiar with the process. I'm further impressed with the book because it is written in plain English and is full of examples that can be easily understood. And I'm sure most witnesses will find the sample transcripts it contains invaluable.

I know there's no such thing as a required reading list for witnesses before they are allowed to give a deposition, but if there were one, *The Deposition Handbook* should be high on the list.

AUTHOR'S PROLOGUE

A few years back, I was reporting a deposition in which the witness was fidgety, histrionic, and even tearful. Several breaks had to be taken to allow him to regain his composure. During one of the breaks, both attorneys left for coffee, and the witness and I stayed in the conference room. At that time, he noticed a magazine I was reading: **"Writer's Digest,"** which led to a discussion about my writing endeavors. He said, "You know, you should write a book on what goes into giving a deposition. In your role as a court reporter, you're a constant observer. You know what goes on, what should or shouldn't be said or done. That's what people like me need to know, then this whole thing wouldn't be so intimidating."

I thought a minute about what he was saying. He was right. The deposition process can be intimidating, mainly because it's not something laypeople are normally familiar with. And even though tens of thousands of people give depositions each year, there are very few books around that acquaint one with the process. To us working in the legal field, there's nothing complicated about the deposition procedure; it's a routine that we go through day in and day out. But for the person being deposed—who stands to gain or lose a lot based on how well she can answer questions—it could lessen the tension if she at least had a guide to refer to for some practical information. Sure, if she has an attorney, the attorney can acquaint her with the process, but attorneys are apt to skim over things simply because they themselves find them routine and basic. And what about the witness who appears at a deposition without an attorney? Wouldn't it be helpful if she at least had some helpful hints?

This book is designed to familiarize the reader with some of the procedures and rules associated with the giving of a deposition. It analyzes, defines, and shows by example the meaning behind some common legal statements made by attorneys during the deposition process, and it also acquaints deponents (those answering the questions) with things they can do to make the process go more smoothly. Additionally, it contains two sample deposition transcripts, which have been included to exemplify how a witness can answer questions so as to add leverage to her position or to show the hazards associated with volunteering too much information.

At this time I'll point out that most of my court reporting experience has been in California, and the rules and statutes governing the deposition procedure vary from state to state. But this in no way limits the book's viability because the rules and examples given herein are general in nature. And from having reviewed the Federal Rules of Civil Procedure and from reporting federal depositions and depositions governed by other states' codes, I haven't discovered any gross variances from what this book contains. Although, the book does contain a internet web address for where you can review the federal rules of discovery and the specific discovery rules that apply to the state or jurisdiction that governs depositions taken in the state where your deposition is being taken. Even though *The Deposition Handbook* contains a wealth of helpful information, please don't think of it as all

inclusive. Law has so many nuances, that there are many terms defining *basically* the same thing. For example, in the text I refer to the "plaintiff" as the party that brings the lawsuit. However, this person could also be called "the applicant," the "petitioner," the "complainant," etc, depending on what type of action is filed. But to have made the book any more detailed would have made it unnecessarily technical and also would have interfered with its simplicity and handiness, which are two of its strengths.

Although (as indicated on the cover) this edition of the book has been updated, I elected to keep it true to its original format—basic, non-technical, and easy to use. However, a few additions have been included: the most notable of which are additions to the chapter commenting on the deposition experiences of Bill Clinton and Bill Gates; a chapter titled "First Things First: Choosing An Attorney who's Right for You"; the inclusion of an additional Sample Transcript that demonstrates how people can mess up when answering questions during depositions; and an Index, making the book even more reader-friendly.

The subtitle of the book is *A Guide To Help You Give A Winning Deposition.* And for those of you who use it, I'm sure you'll find it to be a very qualified guide for helping you achieve that aim.

—oOo—

ACKNOWLEDGMENTS

I am still—18 years since the book's first printing—greatly indebted to the following friends and colleagues for their advice and their support, and their unstinting help in the preparation of this book: Jane Beauchamp, Certified Shorthand Reporter; Nathaniel S. Colley, Jr., retired Attorney at Law; William Jamison, Attorney at Law; VC League (deceased), business advisor; Dale S. Wilson, Attorney at Law; Lisa VanBenthuysen, proofreader; and last—but never least—all the members of ZICA Creative Arts and Literary Guild.

DEPOSITIONS ARE SERIOUS BUSINESS

Depositions are serious business. Take it from the Two Bills; two men who know: Bill Clinton and Bill Gates. Both of these American icons have recently given depositions, and the content of each man's testimony has been criticized. President Clinton has suffered the greatest fallout from his deposition testimony given in the Paula Jones Lawsuit. In a historic ruling made by US District Judge Susan Webber Wright, she said there was "clear and convincing evidence" that during the deposition the President has given "false, misleading and evasive answers that were designed to obstruct the judicial process." As a result, she ordered the President to pay sanctions for legal costs incurred by the Jones' attorneys, and for costs she herself incurred as a result of having to travel to Washington, DC, at the President's request. These fees amounted to approximately $90,000 (which are above and beyond the $850,000 settlement fee he paid to Jones.) And, as we all know, the President's troubles didn't stop there. Judge Wright's ruling started a domino effect, an effect that culminated in President William Jefferson Clinton being the first US president to be impeached (for lying while under oath).

Bill Gates, chairman of Microsoft, Inc., has also given deposition testimony, and US District Judge Thomas Penfield Jackson, who presided over the antitrust proceedings the Federal government initiated against Microsoft, criticized Gates as being evasive during his sworn depositions. According to an Associated Press article appearing in the **"Wall Street Journal"** in November of

1998, these comments were made during a private meeting with the lawyers in the case. Since then, Gates' deposition testimony has appeared on the Microsoft web site, and other legal commentators have expressed the same—if not sharper—opinions. One of the most direct fallouts from Gates' less-than-straightforward testimony was Judge Jackson agreeing with the Government's attorney's need to replay large portions of the video taped deposition. When the Microsoft attorneys argued against the amount of testimony being displayed, the Judge was quoted as saying: "If anything, I think the problem is with your witness [Bill Gates]," not with the way in which the testimony is being presented. He continued, "I think it's evident to every spectator that, for whatever reasons, in many respects Mr. Gates has not been particularly responsive to his deposition interrogation. It's a difficult mix."

As a result of Gate's questionable deposition testimony, Microsoft's most direct consequence was added legal fees and court costs that drawn out legal proceedings can rack up. With Microsoft being the multi-million dollar corporation that it is, such legal costs were most likely considered negligible. But to those with significantly less money (which is most of us) such a fallout can have major financial, legal, and life-altering consequences.

These two scenarios have been presented here to simply make you mindful, that giving a deposition is serious business. So even though the book contains a host of strategies you can use to help stack the cards in your favor, you must be ever mindful of the requirement to be truthful during your deposition. To be less than so would be foolish, because, as you can see, one of the most powerful men in American has suffered serious ramifications [financial loss and impeachment] for not being so. And as for his corporate counterpart, his questionable deposition testimony led to opposing counsel gaining a new tool for chipping away at his credibility and financial interest.

It's worth noting here that both of these powerful men are still faring quite well and were able to rebound nicely, but them being in the highest income brackets afforded them access to other options and opportunities that the average citizen doesn't have. A loss in a lawsuit for someone with fewer financial assets and influential power brokers can spell financial disaster, so adhering to the rules governing deposition testimony is advisable.

—oOo—

FIRST THINGS FIRST:
CHOOSING AN ATTORNEY WHO'S RIGHT FOR YOU

When becoming involved in legal proceedings, deciding whether or not to hire an attorney is one of the first decisions most people make. If you decide to hire one, you should be familiar with some of the following considerations.

- If possible, get a referral from someone you know, like a friend, family member, or some other associate who has used the services of the attorney they're suggesting. That way, they can provide you with some solid information on the pros and cons of using her.

- Local city, county, and state bar associations also make referrals of attorneys. Consult your local phone directory for their phone numbers. Although not as personal, the Internet has numerous data bases that list attorneys. Most of the time, you can find out what kind of law they specialize in and contact them by email to gain more information about them.

- Most attorneys have websites where their biographical information is often posted. By examining their sites, you can find out such things as whether or not they have expertise in the area of law you need, what kind of clients they represent, how long they've been in practice, whether or not they offer a free initial consultation, etc.

- Always schedule an initial consultation. This will enable you to observe how well an attorney listens; if she understands your problem or if she'll have to do research to answer your questions; if she and her staff relate to you in a cordial, professional way; if her office space and materials appear organized; etc.

- Become familiar with how an attorney you're considering using charges for his services. Some charge by the hour and some charge a flat fee. Some charge an initial retainer, and some don't. Find out about costs other than the attorney fees, such as charges for court reporters, transcripts, photocopying, legal research costs, expert witness costs, document service fees, and other out-of-pocket expenses an attorney may occur in handling your case. Also, if an attorney offers to take your case on a contingency fee basis, be real clear on what percentage you'll have to pay him on any judgment or settlement you receive.

- Get some references from the attorney you're considering. These should come from clients she's worked with previously. When you follow up on the contacts she gives you, see if you can get them to remark on her ability to perform in an effective way, and ask them to give you specific examples of what they found likable or admirable about her and what they disliked about her.

- Ask the attorney if he's published any articles or spoke before any groups or organizations. Reading any such articles may give you unfiltered information about the attorney's ethics. Having information about groups or organizations he's spoken before can also shed some light on what his affiliations are. This is one way you can possibly determine if there's a potential clash between significant values you and he stand for.

- Most of the time, nonparties to a lawsuit don't have to have an attorney. However, if you feel you could potentially become a party because of your deposition testimony, then you should strongly consider acquiring the services of an attorney.

The above-mentioned recommendations are helpful, but beyond facts and figures, when you choose an attorney, he should be someone who you feel you can establish a rapport with. Ideally, you and your attorney should work together as a team from start to finish. In an article titled "Hiring a lawyer? 5 questions to ask," (Microsoft.com/small business/resources), author Phillip Harper quotes Suzanne Mishkin of HALT, a Washington, DC—based legal watchdog group, "If an attorney doesn't agree that you should be in the driver's seat, look for someone else." Harper interprets her statement as meaning that the client should monitor all expenses connected with the legal work her attorney does rather than just being a bystander paying the bills after charges have mounted up. The attorney should also explain to you specifically why she deems the legal services are necessary to build your case, so you can make an informed decision about whether or not to authorize extra expenses. In order for an attorney and client to proceed like this effectively, they need a comfortable working relationship with each other. This type of relationship starts with a client choosing the right attorney for her. So also beyond costs and qualifications, you have to examine an attorney's style. This doesn't refer to an attorney's way of dressing or what kind of car he drives. It pertains more to evaluating the attorney's demeanor—how aggressive he presents himself; if he relates to his staff—and other service providers—in a courteous and professional way; if he communicates with you in plain language rather than legal-ease; if he keeps his verbal communication with you on an adult-to-adult level; can he feel any emotional turmoil you may have surrounding the matter, and, if so, can he balance that with his being supportive yet detached? If the money you have available for his services is limited, can he be sensitive to that without making you feel like you're in a lower "class" than he is? The answers to these type questions contribute to one being able to assess an attorney's character. Having some insight into this aspect of him, should give you a gut feeling of whether or not this is a person who you can have a positive and comfortable attorney-client relationship with. Feeling that comfortability is one of the things that will help reduce your stress when giving a deposition and will also supply you with the confidence needed to appropriately seek your attorney's guidance during the proceeding.

For those of you who choose to not hire an attorney and instead represent yourself, perhaps you'll find these words of President Abraham Lincoln encouraging, "If you are resolutely determined to make a lawyer of yourself, the thing is more than half done already."

—oOo—

SOME GENERAL INFORMATION

A deposition is a proceeding whereby you give oral testimony under oath. The proceeding is held sometime before a trial in a civil action. Your testimony consists of the answers you provide to questions an attorney asks you. You're what's known as the "witness," or "deponent." Most depositions are held at law offices, or other business establishments, which makes the setting less formal than when testifying in court, but it has the same force and effect as though testifying in a courtroom before a judge; you're still legally bound to tell the truth.

Throughout the proceeding, the court reporter will record verbatim all the questions and answers, and any other conversation or remarks made by the attorneys. Even if an attorney says "strike that," his statement remains part of the record. The attorneys do have the prerogative of going off the record to discuss certain things, and that discussion is not recorded, but a witness cannot instruct a court reporter to go off the record. The record the reporter produces is the official record of what occurred during the deposition proceeding.

Some depositions are also audio or video taped, but that is not the prevailing practice, and even when they are taped, the expectations or performance of the witness does not change significantly, if at all.

Also, with the assistance of computer technology, oftentimes the deposition proceedings are transcribed instantly and can be readily available to any attorney present. This is made possible through a computer link that a stenographic court reporter can set up with any portable computers attorneys may have brought with them. The utility of the internet has added another dimension to the deposition process, and through a reporter's computerized steno machine interfacing with other computerized devices, deposition testimony can be immediately transported to remote locations. What all this means to the witness is that her testimony can now be instantly scrutinized by others besides the attorneys present, and oftentimes those other attorneys can have input in the deposition proceeding by communicating comments back to the attorneys formulating the deposition questions. At the time of the writing of this book, the use of this technology is not the prevalent practice in depositions that don't involve huge sums of money. Every day, however, computer technology is becoming more and more accessible to the common person, and we're all becoming more computer literate. What this means is attorneys are readily recognizing the conveniences of using such features, so you can expect for them to become more widespread.

—oOo—

SOME KEY LEGAL RIGHTS YOU MAY HAVE

E ven though this book does not give legal advice, there are some basic legal rights that you may have as a deposition witness. Most of these are discussed in layperson's terms throughout the text of the book, but if you desire a more in-depth explanation, you should review the Federal Rules of Civil Procedure, or the Code of Civil Procedure specifically for the state in which the lawsuit has been filed and/or the state in which you'll be deposed. Check for local rules too. These are rules that may be imposed by your local jurisdiction only. Law books containing all of these rules can be found at most public, college, or law libraries.

One book that expands on these rights is *The Deposition Guide*, by Larry G. Johnson, J.D. This book is available for review in its entirety, or you can order a copy, from his website (see References). In particular, this book provides brief synopses on:

- Your right to not incriminate yourself;
- Your attorney-client privilege;
- Your right to a subpoena;
- Your right to a protective order;
- Your right to bring anything that may assist you at your deposition;
- Your right to not answer a question;
- Your right to change an answer after the deposition is over;
- Your right to retain originals of exhibits;
- Your right to nullify or modify a subpoena.

—oOo—

HOW ATTORNEYS USE DEPOSITIONS

The purpose of taking a deposition is for the attorneys, who represent the various parties in a lawsuit, to gather information about a case before a trial. However, after reviewing the information obtained through depositions, they may decide it's better to not go to trial at all and instead will attempt to settle a case.

Take this hypothetical situation:

> Awhile ago, Ms. Jones and Ms. Smith had an automobile accident with each other. Ms. Smith suffered a broken collar bone. She then filed a lawsuit claiming the accident happened because Ms. Jones ran a stop sign. So she is now suing Ms. Jones for a number of damages, including medical bills, costs for car repairs, lost wages because she couldn't work during her recovery period, lost of consortium in her marital relationship because she was unable to fulfill her wifely expectations, and general pain and suffering she experienced during her recuperation period.

However, there are two sides to every story:

> According to Ms. Jones, Ms. Smith is the one who ran the stop sign and caused the accident, and she tells her insurance company this. Her insurance company then as-

signs an investigator and attorney to guide them on how best to handle claim.

This example shows there's a discrepancy between what the involved parties are saying, so through the deposition process the attorneys on each side will attempt to find out what really happened. From the information they receive, through the deposition process or other legal methods, they can assess how strong their case is and make a determination whether it makes more sense to settle the matter out of court or go to trial. If Ms. Jones wants to make a counter claim against Ms. Smith, for her personal damages, she can also hire an attorney to strictly represent her in this matter—not her insurance company. That attorney would then become an equal player in the discovery process.

WHY YOUR DEPOSITION IS BEING TAKEN

You may be deposed for a number of reasons. One is because you are a party to the lawsuit, either you're the person being sued or the person who initiated the lawsuit. Another reason is that you may be a witness to what occurred, either you saw an accident or event happen, or you have personal knowledge or information as to what happened. Such information could be available to you because in your professional capacity you provided a service to one of the parties. For this reason, doctors are deposed quite often. You may also be deposed if you are in possession of documents or records that can substantiate or contradict one or more of the claims in the lawsuit. One other reason for giving a deposition is if you're been retained by one of the attorneys as an expert witness because through your training or experience you have knowledge above and beyond the ordinary layperson's in a certain area or field that's relevant to the lawsuit (more about this later).

It's up to the attorney who wants to conduct the examination to inform witnesses that they are required to give a deposition. This is done in various ways. If you are the plaintiff, the party bringing the lawsuit, you will be informed by a Notice of Deposition that will be sent to your attorney. Because plaintiffs make the initial claims of wrongdoing in a lawsuit and present the foundational information upon which a lawsuit is based, their depositions are usually taken first. If you are the defendant, the party alleged to have committed an offense, you will receive a notice, or maybe even a subpoena, compelling you to appear and testify. If you are an employee of a business that's being sued at the time of the filing of the lawsuit, you too can be subpoenaed or noticed to give deposition testimony. If you are just a percipient witness (a witness uninvolved in the lawsuit but who can substantiate or refute one or more of the claims in the matter), your attendance can also be required by a subpoena. Most of the other participants are usually just noticed that the deposition is being held, and they may attend if they desire. And many times deposition witnesses aren't served with any type of legal documents compelling their appearance, but instead are deposed because the involved attorneys have stipulated to do so.

THINGS TO KEEP IN MIND BEFORE
BEING DEPOSED

When writing this chapter, a spiritual principle in a book compiled by E. Peters, *African Openings to the Tree of Life*, which is traced to Guinean wisdom, came to mind: "To make preparations does not spoil the trip." Truer words have never been spoken when it comes to the deposition process. Here are some things you may want to do to prepare:

- Find out how long the deposition is expected to go so you can make arrangements to have your other responsibilities or commitments covered and won't have to be concerned about them when giving your testimony. But keep in mind that whatever time estimate you're given is only the attorneys' best estimate, and depositions have been know to go way beyond their estimated time. They can also be shorter than expected.

- Review any written materials that you believe may be pertinent in refreshing your recollection, but beware if you do that the examining attorney can question you about your review of any documents you reviewed. So if you do feel there's something you would like to review, check with your attorney beforehand to see whether he thinks it's advisable. You can also be questioned about other people you may have conversed with about the case. And, you can even be questioned about your reading of this book.

- Also, keep in mind that if you do divulge to the deposing attorney that you reviewed any notes or other materials to prepare for the deposition, she has a right to request that your materials are marked as an exhibit to the deposition. If you want to keep your original notes or other materials, your attorney can request that a copy of them be made and that the copy is marked instead. That way you can retain your original materials. If your original materials are marked, and are taken by the court reporter, your attorney should have the deposing attorney agree, on the record, that you can have your original materials back—ideally once they are copied, or, less preferably, once the case is resolved.

- Try to be well rested and relaxed, and abstain from using alcohol or any other substances that may alter your ability to recollect the facts or events. However, if you are under medication that may interfere with your testimony, and that medication has been medically prescribed, check with your physician and get her advice as to whether or not you can safely skip taking it until after you've finished testifying. Any advisement she gives you that may interfere with your testimony should be relayed to your attorney.

- Dress comfortable. Don't wear shoes that hurt or a tie that chokes. Your attire should be appropriate to your station in life, but it should also be something you're at ease in when wearing it. An opposing attorney may be forming opinions based on your appearance in attempting to determine the type of impression you may make before a jury or judge, so appearance can be important. This is especially true if the deposition will be video-taped. If you need glasses or a hearing aid, make sure to bring them. Depositions have been adjourned and rescheduled because the witness was not prepared with what she needed to participate in the process. This causes an inconvenience to the attorneys and all others in attendance, and it is also something you might be billed for if you're a party to the lawsuit.

- If you fail to appear at the deposition, you may be charged with contempt of a court order. If you're the plaintiff in the lawsuit and you fail to appear, your claim might get dismissed due to your failure. Oftentimes there are legitimate reasons a person fails to appear, so if this happens to you, make sure you have a valid and, if possible, verifiable justification.

- Arrive early to allow time to unwind or discuss any last-minute things with your attorney. If you do arrive early and your attorney is not there yet, don't discuss the case or your anticipated testimony with others who may be there. You may not know whose side they're on or what key information you might be giving up.

- Many times attorneys bill by the hour for their time, so try not to be late. If you're going to be so late as to delay the deposition starting time considerably, the attorneys may want to reschedule the proceeding.

—oOo—

OTHERS WHO MAY BE PRESENT

Overall, depositions are closed proceedings, allowing only the involved parties or those ordered to be there to be present. As previously mentioned, the advent of the internet has somewhat broadened the term "present," in the sense that a transcript of the proceedings (and often even a video) of what is presently occurring at the deposition can be transmitted to remote computers at other locations. In most jurisdictions for this to happen, though, the involved attorneys have to stipulate to the transmission. As a rule of thumb, though, the usual persons present are:

- Any party to the lawsuit, on any side;

- Your attorney and at least one opposing attorney (an attorney representing another party in the lawsuit). If you are not a party to the lawsuit, then you may not need an attorney there to represent you; however, if you feel that testimony you may give may tend to implicate you in the matter (or in some other way harm you), then you may want your attorney there to advise you;

- An insurance company representative if the lawsuit involves a person/party covered by an insurer, or a union representative if a labor union is involved.

- Miscellaneous others, which may include: an interpreter, if one of the parties speaks a language other than English; a video recorder operator, if the parties have all agreed to make a video recording of the proceedings; the parents of a minor child, if the child is testifying or is a party to the lawsuit; an attorney's law partner or associate, or legal assistant; the spouse of the person testifying; an aide for a disabled participant.

- From time to time, attorneys may agree to allow various others in, but this doesn't happen too often.

RECORDING THE PROCEEDINGS

A court reporter will be present at the deposition. A court reporter is an officer of the court and is trained to record oral proceedings verbatim. The prevailing method for doing this is by use of a steno machine. Overall, court reporters are highly trained and are quite competent in the performance of their duties. The court reporter is also the one who usually administers the oath to a witness. In any deposition, even when a court reporter may have been hired by an opposing party in the litigation, she is required, by law, to be impartial and disinterested in the issues pertaining to the outcome of the lawsuit. In fact, many attorneys talk openly to their clients about confidential matters in the presence of court reporters. However, if you're uncomfortable with your attorney doing this, you should inform him. A legal reason to be concerned about attorneys doing this is it could possibly violate the attorney-client privilege. Attorney-client privilege generally means that anything you and your attorney tell each other in confidence becomes privileged information, meaning it isn't required to be divulged to others during the legal proceedings. If such information is broadcast to a third-party, an opposing attorney may be able to question a deponent about it because the privilege was violated.

Before going on the record, most likely the court reporter will ask you for your name, mailing address, and phone number. Usually she asks witnesses to sit close to her to make sure she can hear their testimony correctly. Also, the closer you are to her, the easier it is for her to ask you to repeat something you've said that she's unsure about, or to spell a word. And if you speak too rapidly, she may also ask you to slow down. For the most part, court reporters don't talk a lot during depositions, but if more than one person talks at a time, or arguments erupt, or the proceedings start to get generally unruly, the reporter has a professional obligation to interrupt to help restore the order she needs to make an accurate record of what is being spoken.

At the request of one of the parties involved, sometimes deposition proceedings are videotaped. One of the advantages to videotaping a deposition is that it can give other key participants in the legal proceeding, who are not present, a chance to view the actual behavior and facial expressions of those physically at the deposition. A written transcript doesn't provide this type information. A drawback to videotaping is that it usually adds considerably to the charges for the proceeding. In most jurisdictions even if a deposition is being video taped, a certified shorthand reporter will still be there, and, oftentimes, she's the same person that will do the video recording. This can be particularly helpful should the matter proceed to trial, because from a written transcript that a stenographic reporter would prepare, attorneys can find far quicker those portions of a witness's testimony that they want to call attention to. Also, with the advent of computer-aided stenographic reporting, oftentimes attorneys can receive an instant transcript of the proceedings, and the entire text can be searched and cross-referenced by computer. Court reporters who produce transcripts in such a timely way use a skill called "real time." Not all court reporters are trained to do it, so a real time reporter would have to be requested when the deposition is scheduled. However, when attorneys are trying to adhere to court-ordered time lines for their legal processes, having an instant transcript can be of great advantage to them and their clients.

Even if an instant transcript is not produced, some time after the deposition is concluded, the court reporter will contact you if she prepared a transcript of the proceedings. At that time she will inform you of how many days you have to appear at her office if you wish to review and sign it. The number of days a deponent is given to appear for the review and signing of a deposition transcript varies from jurisdiction to jurisdiction—however, it's usually 30 days or less. If for some reason you don't review and sign your transcript, it will be accepted as an accurate transcription of your words. It can then be used at a trial or other proceedings. Although, from time to time, a witness's attorney may take actions to try and bar the use of an un-reviewed transcript. Attorneys also try to accommodate their expert witnesses and often make stipulations on the record that a transcript can be mailed to an expert. This is usually a cost-saving agreement because experts are apt to charge their hourly professional rate if they have to travel to review a deposition transcript. The use of electronic signatures, where a person signs a form on an Internet website, is becoming more of a practice when signing legal documents. For example, state and federal tax returns are often signed this way. Some states may even allow deposition transcripts to be reviewed remotely and validated by witness through this process. You can ask your attorney or the court reporter, or you can check your state and local rules of civil procedure to see if they address this practice (also see pages 74-75).

—oOo—

THE FIRST FEW STATEMENTS
ON THE RECORD

U sually as soon as the deposing attorney starts his examination, he will seek to get some background information from you, such as your name and address, age, where you go or went to school, your place of employment, whether or not you're married or have a family. Most likely he'll also introduce himself and inform you who he represents. He may even mention that he's not there to trick or trap you (however, use your own best judgment as to whether or not you believe something he says is misleading.) Next, he will probably inform you of some ground rules he considers important to the deposition process.

Some Standard Ground Rules

- You've been placed under oath to tell the truth, and that oath has the same effect and consequences as if you're testifying in a court of law.

- When taking the oath, if you prefer not to *swear* to tell the truth, it's okay to *affirm* to do so.

- If you don't know an answer, can't recall, or can't remember information, say so. Those are perfectly acce ceptable answers. But if you have a best estimate or approximation, the attorney is entitled to receive that information.

- Answer audibly. Avoid saying "uh-huh" and "uhn-uhn," shaking or nodding your head, shrugging your shoulders, and other gestures or guttural responses. A deposition is an oral recording, and definitive verbal responses are required in order to make a clear record.

- You can take a short comfort break—washroom, coffee, whatever. Just ask, and usually it will be complied with immediately or within a few minutes.

- If you need to stop the proceeding to confer privately with your attorney, that's also permissible. Just say that's what you need to do, and your attorney will usually tell the court reporter to go off the record. An opposing attorney may balk at this, and may even comment about it on the record, but he can't deny you this right.

- If you don't understand a question, say so. It's the examining attorney's duty to reframe or reword the question until it's understandable to you. You could be doing yourself, or the case, a great disservice if you answer a question that you don't fully understand.

- Wait until an attorney asking a question has fully finished the question before you start to answer. That way you're sure exactly what question you're answering. You also need to wait because a stenographic court reporter can't record two people talking at the same time. Even a reporter making an audio or video recording of proceedings would prefer to not have people talking over each other because when that occurs the recording comes out garbled. Of course, this works both ways; the attorney should also allow you to finish your answer before he asks you the next question.

- Be prepared to be asked about the possibility of your being under the influence of drugs (prescription or otherwise) or alcohol. As previously mentioned, such substances may affect your ability to testify effectively. The attorney may probe further into this area by asking if there is anything at all to preclude you from giving your best testimony.

- You have a right to make changes to your deposition once the transcript is completed. However, if you make a significant change, or a lot of changes, then an opposing attorney may comment on that if the case goes to trial. For instance, during a person's deposition testimony they may be asked how many beers they had to drink within two hours before an accident, and they may say "a six pack," and then later on when they're reviewing their deposition transcript, they may change the answer to "two beers." Well, if the case goes to trial, an opposing attorney may, to undermine their credibility, call attention to such a change. Likewise, if you change a "yes" answer to a "no," or change any answer to its opposite, that can prove to be just as harmful if brought out at trial. Therefore, pay close attention to all questions asked so as to minimize any changes you may need to make at a later time. One other thing to keep in mind in this regard is that your attorney can assist you in the review of your deposition transcript.

- If you do misspeak or answer incorrectly and realize it during the deposition, you can clarify or correct your previous answer right during the deposition by saying you misspoke. Just tell the questioning attorney, or your own attorney, that you need to change or clarify something you said earlier.

SOME BASICS ABOUT ANSWERING QUESTIONS

To repeat:

> It appears to me that in Ethics, as in all
> other philosophical studies, the difficulties
> and disagreements, of which history is full,
> are mainly due to a very simple cause:
> namely, to attempt to answer questions,
> without first discovering precisely what
> question it is which you desire to answer.

> **~ Principia Ethica [1903] ~**
> **George Edward Moore**

In other words:

- Take your time. It's okay to think a few seconds before answering.

- Answer concisely. Don't volunteer additional information. If a question calls for a yes or no answer, you
  should answer as such. But if after answering you feel
  you need to explain your answer, then you have that
  right. Keep in mind, though, your explanation could
  divulge information the questioning attorney is not entitled to. If your attorney detects that happening, he
  may interject and say something like, "you've already
  answered the question." That's a warning for you to
  stop. Sometimes before you even start to respond to

the question, your attorney may interject "if you know." If he does that, he probably doesn't want you to answer in too much detail, or he's advising you that the information you've been asked to provide may be something he believes you may not have personal knowledge of. If you feel his admonition is warranted, it may be better for you to say you don't know rather than speculating or guessing.

- Looking at your attorney for guidance. Sometimes witnesses look at their attorneys if they're seeking direction when answering a particular question, and the attorney may say go ahead if you can answer it. An example comes to mind of a witness who did that several times during a deposition. As a result, the questioning attorney got upset and let her know, rather smugly, that he didn't appreciate her looking at her attorney before answering his questions. The witness got irate and told him—in no uncertain terms—that she could look at anyone whom she pleased to look at, and she wasn't going to let him or anyone else tell her she couldn't. The attorney backed off, and throughout the rest of the deposition the witness looked at her attorney whenever she was hesitant about answering a question. <u>However, your attorney (nor anyone else) can't outright answer a question for you.</u> At times, though, he may assist you by clarifying a question or informing the questioning attorney of the reason you're having difficulty answering a particular question.

- Hearsay is allowed in depositions. If you have information on something the attorney is asking you about, but you got the information from somebody else, it's okay to divulge the information. Most likely, the examining attorney will just ask who told you or how you know. On the other hand, the attorney may limit his question to "your personal knowledge." In that case, tell only what you yourself heard or experienced firsthand. There may be times when you're testifying about what someone else said and the attorney will ask you for the exact words that were used. If you can remember them, give him the words as exactly as you can, even if the words are profane. If you can't remember the exact words, you may want to preface your answer with something like, "This is as close as I can recall, but it's not exact."

- Give your best estimate or recollection about facts or events. However, if you have doubts about the accuracy of your estimate or recollection, be sure to preface your answer with a phrase or words such as "I think so; that seems about right; as best I can recall; as far as I remember, but I'm not exactly certain; about; around; generally; sometimes; from what I could tell; yes, but…" and so forth and so on.

- If you feel a question that's asked you is too invasive into your private life, or is too unconnected to the issues of the lawsuit, you can point this out to your attorney. However, you still may be required to answer the question because attorneys have wide latitude with their questions during discovery (exceptions to this will be covered in the section, "If You're Instructed Not to Answer.")

- Speak clearly, at a moderate level and pace. Even

though the court reporter is usually silent during the deposition proceeding, she may have to interrupt the testimony from time to time to ask you to repeat an answer. This usually occurs for one of the following reasons:

- If you have a heavy accent or unusual speech pattern;
- If you're using esoteric, medical or technical terms;
- If she doesn't hear or understand you because you're speaking too softly;
- If you are talking too fast or speaking un-clearly.

- If you are asked to repeat something, you should re-peat the answer using the same, or close to the same, words you used the first time you said it. Also, if you use a proper or technical name she's not familiar with, she may ask for the spelling.

- Joking and wise-cracking should be avoided because once such remarks are reduced to written words, they can easily be misinterpreted and possibly be used against you. Some attorneys are aware that this can happen and may make an immediate statement on the record that the witness was joking when she said that.

—oOo—

CROSS-EXAMINATION

Cross-examination in a deposition is when you are a witness for one side in a lawsuit, and an attorney representing another side questions you. Deposition cross-examination differs from that at trial in many respects. Cross-examination at trial usually follows the direct examination of the attorney who called the witness to testify, and his questions are usually limited to those areas opened up on direct examination (the witness' initial testimony). Cross-examination at a deposition is usually the opening examination, and the area of questioning covers a wide scope.

During cross-examination at a deposition, the examining attorney is probably not only making note of the answers he receives, but may also be paying attention to your nonverbal behavior, such as fluctuation in your tone of voice; when you hesitate; what makes you upset; how you behave, if you're jittery; when you repeat things unnecessarily (which may indicate you've been coached in a certain area), etc. Also, cross-examination during the deposition process is generally not as harsh and theatrical as it sometimes is in court. An opposing attorney may even come across as a friend or supporter. He's usually rather accommodating. It's to his advantage to be this way because it usually makes a witness feel relaxed and unguarded about divulging the information he's trying to gather.

Many questions asked during cross-examination may seem trivial and insignificant; and, individually they may well be. But keep in mind that when seemingly insignificant facts are added together, they can lay a damaging foundation.

If questions are put to you during cross-examination that concern something you have strong feelings about, as much as possible remain calm. Mouthing off a biting retort can be sweet, but, remember, it can also be damaging. It's best to not lose your composure and spout off things that can later hurt your case, or your credibility. And although your attorney can always do a follow-up examination of you himself and try to undo any mistakes you may have made due to being upset, he still can't strike the words you uttered from the record.

At times during cross-examination a witness may find herself in an awkward situation and may resort to lying, even though she's taken an oath to tell the truth. During the deposition the questioning attorney may be aware this is happening but he may purposely not confront a witness about it at that time. At a trial in the matter, however, is when he's apt to confront the witness about it, because it's usually at a trial when attorneys attack witnesses on bad faith, lack of honesty, hypocrisy, treachery, carelessness, double-dealing, or other unscrupulous conduct. That's when it is far more damaging and more likely to add leverage to his side of the lawsuit.

Cross-Examination Strategies

- Questions can be phrased in a way to elicit a desired response. For example, can you imagine an employer who has been accused of racially prejudicial employment practices answering yes to this question: Do you disagree that qualified minorities should be given the same opportunities for promotion that their white counterparts have?

- Many times attorneys already know the answers to questions they ask during cross-examination, but they ask them anyway to lay a foundation or get a witness to state information that may be damaging to her. If an attorney has been repeatedly asking the same question, although slightly rewording it each time, and then he suddenly stops and moves on to a different area, it may mean he finally got a desirable answer to support a contention favorable to his side in the lawsuit. If you are able to remember this area of questioning, you may want to ask your attorney about it later, perhaps during a break in the deposition so as to allow him time to revisit that issue if necessary.

- Oftentimes, questions are asked in the negative to give the impression that the attorney has already verified the information he's asking for. Such a question can make the witness feel it's in her best interest to agree or be caught in a lie. An example of such a question is: Didn't you tell Mr. Watson you have information about the corporation's hiring practices? Asking a question in the negative is an effective ploy, but it's not necessarily a fact that the attorney has the information he's led you to believe he has.

- Another tactic during cross-examination is to phrase a question so as to give you a choice of two answers, but neither of the answers offered is that favorable. Take, for example, a hypothetical situation of a woman who took out a loan and as collateral gave the lender the pink slip to her car. When the woman defaulted on the loan, and the lender had to seek legal action to collect the debt, it came out during cross-examination that previous to the loan being made title to the car had been transferred to the woman's father. The question the attorney asked was: Well, ma'am, since it's now clear you're unable to pay back your debt, who do you plan to cheat, my client or your father?

Just because a question is phrased in an either-or manner, you're not required to answer it from that perspective. A witness always has the right to ask the questioning attorney to rephrase a question.

- When your involvement in something unfavorable or unsavory is brought up, but it's something you truly didn't know about, or didn't know would be harmful or detrimental to others, and you're now finding this out for the first time, it's okay to display your astonishment. Your reaction may be a convincing expression of sincerity and could alter favorably the other side's opinion of your culpability.

- If a letter or other document that might compromise your position is presented, and it's something you've signed, it may be unwise to disavow having knowledge of it. But you may be able to save face if you're next asked if you read and understood it before signing. If you have an attorney (or other professional) who advises you on your affairs, an acceptable answer to that question may be: Maybe I didn't read it that carefully because I pay my attorney to review these types of things and advise me on them.

- When a question is asked, and a phrase like "is that correct" or "is that right" is added to the end of the question, the question is calling for a yes or no answer. But when answering, you have watch out for double meanings. For example:

  Q. You didn't lock your car when you parked it; is that correct?
  A. No.

  Does your answering no mean you didn't lock your car when you parked it, or does it mean that *your attorney's statement* that you didn't lock my car when you parked it is not correct? In other words, whether or not you locked the car depends on which part of the question you're responding to. Attorneys phrase their questions like this often, so be clear in your answer which part of the question you're responding to.

- Questions that contain descriptive phrases and words like the following: frequently, slightly, often, fast, a lot, a small amount, sometimes, a few, etc. oftentimes aren't definitive because these words mean different things to different people. If you're answering about something that's pertinent to your case and you feel that the attorney's question isn't specific enough, then make sure that your answer is as specific as need be to support your position on something. Of course, you or your attorney can always ask the questioning attorney to rephrase his question so that it is more definitive.

—oOo—

EMOTIONAL REACTIONS

"Anyone can be angry—that is easy. But to be angry with the right person, to the right degree, at the right time, for the right purpose, and in the right way—that is not easy."

~ Aristotle, *The Nichomachen Ethics* ~

Sometimes a witness gets emotional during a deposition, wants to cry or yell or whatever. Crying is usually tolerated. Yelling is frowned upon. Breaks are usually taken if you need to cry; however, if you get into a yelling match with the examining attorney, he may somehow make an unfavorable reference to that in the transcript of the proceedings. Such a reference can end up hurting your character should you later have to testify before a judge or jury. So it's paramount that you display your emotions as appropriately as possible.

On the other hand, attorneys from time to time yell at each other during depositions. However, when it happens between them, it's usually more tolerated because they're the ones in control of the deposition procedure. Sometimes attorneys even yell at their clients if a client answers incorrectly or gives up too much information. If this happens to you, and it makes you feel uncomfortable, then speak up and tell your attorney to get a grip on his behavior. A practical way to handle this is to request a break so you can tell the attorney off the record, in private, about his inappropriate behavior. If you feel somewhat intimidated by your counsel's behavior and position, just keep in mind that your attorney's professional commitment to guide you through the deposition process does not give him license to treat you like a misbehaving child. This advice also applies to any other attorney who may deal with you in a less than courteous manner (except in this case, you'd have to express your complaint in the presence of the other participants rather than privately).

Another reason for remaining as calm as possible during a deposition is that if your emotions become too intense, it can make it harder for you to think and answer accurately. Gary Goleman talks about this in his book *Emotional Intelligence* when he says, "For better or worse, intelligence can come to nothing when the emotions hold sway." So even if an attorney is delving into matters that evoke strong feelings in you, it is to your advantage to control your emotions. And remember, you can always ask for a short recess if you feel you need to regain your composure.

Other researchers, such as Joshua Freedman, also talk about managing our emotions as a sign of our intelligence. In Freedman's book *Handle With Care: Emotional Intelligence Activity Book,* when he—along with his co-authors (Anabel Jensen, Ph.D., Marsha Rideout, and Patricia Freedman)—states: Emotional intelligence is a way or recognizing, understanding, and choosing how we think, feel, and act. It shapes our interactions with others and our understanding of ourselves. It defines how and what we learn; it allows us to set priorities; it determines the majority of our daily actions. **Research suggests it is *responsible for as much as 80% of the 'success' in our lives.*** Accepting this, since giving deposition testimony presents a situation where a party to a lawsuit most likely desires to be successful, exercising your ability to display your emotions—in an effective way—should contribute favorably to a desirable outcome.

OBJECTIONS

An objection is a verbal expression of opposition. Attorneys raise objections because they deem a question (or answer) is improper, or because they want to exclude from the deposition record information they feel is not relevant to the issues.

When an objection is made, wait a second or two before you start to answer because your attorney, or any other attorney present, may want to make a statement for the record that's connected to the objection. You can then go ahead and answer the question unless your attorney instructs you not to (more about this later).

Objections can lead to arguments between the attorneys. You should stay out of these arguments (or discussions) because most of the time they are based on legal issues a layperson is not familiar enough with to comment on.

Sometimes if an objection is made, the examining attorney will reword the question or explain it more, to make sure the question is clear and/or the objecting attorney considers it appropriate. Sometimes he won't reword it. He'll just ask the witness if she understands, disregarding whether or not the other attorney understands or accepts the question. In these instances, if the attorney representing the witness being examined is the one objecting, the witness can support her attorney and say something like, "I don't understand. Will you please restate it." But sometimes a witness will just say yes, she understands, and proceed to answer the question. This leaves her attorney having to fend for himself and it also leads to the witness possibly answering an improper question. Asking the attorney to reword his question is the more favorable response because it demonstrates to all present that you and your attorney are working as a team in this matter.

Frequently Raised Objections

- **Compound**. This means an attorney has asked at least two different questions in one, and his question might therefore call for more than one answer.

  For example:
  Q   Did you lock your door and set your burglar alarm before you left your apartment?

  The witness' attorney would probably ask the questioning attorney to ask about locking the door in one question and about setting the alarm in another.

- **Vague and ambiguous**. It's not clear what the question is asking for. It may not include a needed word or description that's needed for it to be understood. Or the attorney may have misspoken in his phrasing of the question. Therefore, it is hard for the witness to answer the question.

  For example:
  Q   Okay, you've just explained how this accident happened. Now I want to know how fast you were traveling?

  It's not clear from the question if the attorney means how fast the witness was going when she first saw the vehicle she collided with, how fast just before the collision, how fast at the time of impact, how fast after impact. The witness' attorney will probably ask the questioning attorney to be more specific before she's allowed to answer the question.

- **Leading and suggestive.** This one happens mainly if a witness answers a question one way and her attorney attempts to clarify, or enhance, the answer, and in doing so adds information that makes the witness answer in a specific way. If this happens, the examining attorney may say something like "I object to you leading the witness."

For example:
MR. SCOTT: It only takes a few minutes to get to Wanda's school from your house; is that correct?
THE WITNESS: Yes.
MR. SCOTT: So you would not have had to stop and get gas on your way, right?
MR. MILLER: Objection, counsel. She hasn't told us the reason she didn't stop for gas. I object to you leading the witness.

Another example:
MR. SCOTT: Now, Vivian, you said you didn't fill out the "Request for Time Off." Is that because you had previously told Miss Watkins in a meeting that you would be taking time off for your doctor's appointments, and she said that was fine?
MR. MILLER: Objection. Counsel, I strenuously object to you leading your own witness.

THE DEPOSITION HANDBOOK

- **Incomplete hypothetical.** These questions oftentimes start off with something like "let's suppose."
The attorney then gives a possible scenario of how or
why something happened and/or what material things
were need to make something happen. Then he'll say
something like "does that affect your answer?" If all
the necessary elements aren't included in the scenario, or one of the elements changes the original
question that the witness previously answered, the
witness' attorney, or another opposing counsel, may
object that it's an incomplete hypothetical.

  For example:
  Q   Now, if there would have been a gate at the head
  of the path leading to the lake, Amanda would not
  have been able to get to the water; is that correct?
      MR. MILLER: Objection, incomplete hypotheti-
  cal. You haven't included whether or not the gate was
  locked or how high the gate would be.

- **Asked and answered.** This means the question was
already asked and the witness has already answered
it. Her attorney may not want her to answer again because if the answer is not exactly the same as the first
time, because if the case were to go to trial, the opposing attorney could possibly use that against her by
pointing out that she gave inconsistent statements.

- **Object to the answer as nonresponsive, ask that it
be stricken.** This objection may be made by the attorney doing the examination rather than the witness'
attorney. It's usually made when a witness either did
not provide a relevant answer to the question being

asked, or she added too many other facts in her answer. The added information may help her case, but it's not information the attorney asked for. As previously mentioned, the answer will continue to be part of the deposition transcript, but the objecting attorney is preserving his right to ask a judge to strike the answer at a later time.

For example:

Q   Did you pay Mr. Lincoln for the car you purchased from him, the $5000 you agreed to pay him?

A   Mr. Lincoln owes me money. That rattletrap he sold me started falling apart from the day I drove it off the lot.

- **Misstates prior testimony.** This is usually an objection made against a question asked by the examining attorney, when his present question attempts to sum up things that were previously stated, but he doesn't state them exactly as given by the witness.

For example:

Q   Now, the only reason you've given for Mr. Corklin not liking overweight people is that he didn't promote you to the position of sales manager.

And what I want I want to know is—

MR. MILLER: Objection. Misstates prior testimony.

MR. SCOTT: That's what she said. I have it in my notes.

MR. MILLER: Yes, but she stated that she also arrived at that conclusion because during 1998 and '99 only four people were terminated, and all of them were significantly overweight.

- **Badgering.** This means in trying to elicit his answer, the examining attorney's tone, demeanor, or tactics are confrontational or overbearing.

  For example
  Q   You were at the Neon Bar that night, weren't you?
  A   I don't know.
  Q   Well, that was a Friday. You're usually there on Fridays, aren't you?
  A   Yes, but
  Q   Just answer the question. I don't want an explanation.
  A   What I'm trying to say is—
  Q   I don't want to know what you're trying to say. I just want a yes or no answer. Can't you understand English—
   MR. MILLER: Objection, badgering the Witness.
   Counsel, you're way out of line.

- **Overbroad.** This objection means the question isn't specific enough. The attorney needs to be more limited in what he's asking the witness to reply to.

  For example:
  Q   Have you ever had an accident where you sustained an injury?
   MR. MILLER: Objection. Don't answer that.
   Do you mean automobile accidents, falling off a bike as a child, cutting her hand while chopping vegetables?
   As phrased, the question is overbroad.

- **Beyond the scope of the witness' knowledge.** This means the witness has no way of answering this question because she has no facts, knowledge, or other information to enable her to make an informed or true response.

For example:

Q   Now, you say your wife was under a lot of stress while working in Wichard's purchasing department. Is that because Mr. Falstaff was an ineffective supervisor?

MR. MILLER: Objection. This witness has no way of rating Mr. Falstaff's supervising abilities. You can ask him what his wife told him about how she thinks Mr. Falstaff contributed to her stress, but not how he rates Mr. Falstaff as a supervisor.

- **Asks for speculation.** This objection is close to the previous one. Perhaps the main difference is this one is usually made when an attorney is asking a witness to answer a question based on what someone else may be thinking or feeling, or what may have motivated someone else to do or not do something, and the witness has no way of knowing that.

For example:

Q   Do you think Ms. Reynolds considered the hardship it would cause these employees if their salary was cut in half?

MR. MILLER: Objection, counsel, you're asking her to speculate as to what was in Ms. Reynolds' head. I'm not going to let her answer that.

* **Violates attorney-client privilege.** The subject of communications between an attorney and his client is confidential and is protected by what's called attorney-client privilege. If a question asked by an examining attorney would require a witness to divulge such communications, the witness' attorney can object to the witness answering the question for that reason. Oftentimes a witness' attorney may allow the witness to answer the question if part of the information the questioning attorney is seeking could have come from some other source.

    For example:
    Q   Has anyone told you that the Witchard Corporation has filed for bankruptcy?

    MR. MILLER: Objection, violates attorney-client privilege.

    Don't answer the question.

    MR. SCOTT: I mean other than what you may have told her.

    MR. MILLER: Go ahead, you can answer now.

* **Objection to the witness drawing a sketch or diagram.** Sometimes the examining attorney may ask a witness to draw a diagram or sketch. The witness' attorney may object to this because such drawings are normally not to scale and often do no accurately reflect the location of items or objects in question. Because of this, attorneys are sometimes apprehensive about the diagram possibly being used at a later time to attack a witness' recollection of a scene or events.

VIRGINIA A. LATHAN

****

Even though this section has focused mainly on a witness that's being represented by an attorney, many of these same objections are raised even when an un-represented witness is being examined, such as a percipient witness, and even when an expert witness is being examined.

—oOo—

IF YOU'RE INSTRUCTED NOT TO ANSWER

As a general rule, you're required to answer all proper questions you're asked. At times, witnesses who have felt pressured to divulge something, that they truly would rather not, have given noncommittal or evasive answers. But, nevertheless, they still have answered. However, if it's evident that a witness is answering in such a way so as to be obstructive to the deposition process, the examining attorney has a right to set a hearing and have a judge examine her responses. And, depending on the degree she determines the witness' evasiveness is outright obstructiveness, she can impose on her a fine or other penalties.

There are times when a witness' attorney will instruct her not to answer due to some legal reason. If this happens, the examining attorney may ask the witness directly if she's refusing to answer the question. The witness can then say yes or no. But if this happens to you and your attorney has instructed you not to answer, then I recommend you follow his advice. The attorney may be giving this instruction because the question has been asked and answered already, because your answering it may divulge information you gained from him, or for any of the other reasons indicated in the section of this book that covered objections.

Although different jurisdictions handle a witness's refusal to answer in different ways, a common practice is for the examining attorney to tell the court reporter, who's an office of the Court, to instruct the witness to answer the question. If that happens, the reporter will usually read the question and then ask the witness to answer it. But this is just to make things official, and you should still follow your attorney's instructions in this regard.

If an attorney is adamant about getting an answer, then he may tell the court reporter to certify the question, which means, at that point in time, he plans to have the witness appear in law and motion court and have the judge instruct her to answer the question. From information I have gathered, it's rare that attorneys carry the process this far, but it is a legal recourse they have for getting the information they want. If things do evolve to this point and a judge orders you to answer, you can be held in contempt of court if you still refuse to answer. However, an exception to this outcome is if your answering the question would incriminate you, because then your constitutional right may entitle you not to have to answer it. Keep in mind, however, even though you may be constitutionally protected from being required to answer, depending on the nature of the lawsuit, you could possibly experience other undesirable consequences for not complying.

THE EXPERT WITNESS

The expert witness is a person, who, through training, education, and/or experience, is qualified to make certain judgments or assumptions about the facts in a case. If you are retained as an expert witness by one side or the other, you will be expected to substantiate or refute claims in the lawsuit. What follows are some things to keep in mind if you'll be giving expert witness testimony.

- You will be questioned about your qualifications, education, experience and publications. It would be helpful if you bring a copy of your curriculum vitae with you, because many times attorneys like to attach them to the deposition transcript as an exhibit. That way his examination of your qualifications to give expert opinions can flow more smoothly.

- Be prepared to recite the names of any attorneys and law firms you have been retained by previously, and also be able to give a breakdown as to whether they were plaintiff or defense firms. Also be ready to give a brief summation of what the lawsuits involved and indicate whether the elements of the case were similar to the one you're currently being deposed about.

- Be mindful of any former opinions you may have expressed that may conflict with your opinions in the present case. For example, if the elements of the current case are similar to those of a case you testified in previously, and you were testifying as a defense expert then and a plaintiff's expert now, you should be prepared to point out the variances in the two cases so as to substantiate your current opinions.

- Be prepared to identify any written materials you used, or reviewed, in formulating your opinions in the present case.

- Be prepared to explain and defend your assumptions and conclusions that substantiate your opinions in this case.

- Be prepared to identify any of your colleagues with whom you may have discussed your assumptions or opinions.

- You will be asked to divulge the specific issues you were asked to examine or consider that pertain to this case. This may also include presenting information on physical things, i.e. the scene of an accident, the reliability of a piece of equipment, what behavior should be expected of a reasonable or normal person; the functionability of an injured person, etc.

- Expect to state your fee for testifying in court and for giving a deposition. Also, if you've charged the attorney who hired you anything for preparation time or other expenses you incurred, be prepared to divulge those amounts also. Most experts require attorneys to prepay them before they give deposition testimony. This way, even if a lawsuit is dropped, they'll be sure of getting paid for the time and work they spent preparing for the deposition testimony.

- If you put together a file pertaining to the case, any attorney involved in the case has a right to examine it. One of the attorneys may even have the court reporter mark it (or selected items from it) as an exhibit and attach it to the deposition transcript. If this happens, you are entitled to retain your original copy of the file, and copies made from it should be attached to the transcript. Actually, once the file has been marked, the attorneys can arrange for a copy service to come to your office and copy it, so your original file never has to leave your custody.

- Even though expert witnesses are almost always deposed by attorneys who represent the opposite side of the attorney who retained you, you should expect the attorney who retained you to interject questions from time to time. When this happens, pay attention to his drift, because he's usually attempting to clarify something you've said, or even attempting to get you to restate something you've testified about in a way that's more favorable to the side he represents in the lawsuit.

- Always keep in mind this fact when being examined by an opposing attorney: He will be attempting to show the facts you have are inadequate for any conclusions you've reached that benefit the side of the attorney who retained you. This attack on your expertise can be derived at through him showing you are not properly qualified to present an opinion or by pointing out weaknesses in your theory as to how a condition or event occurred.

- Remember the phrase "reasonable probability." That's what you'll be aiming to show when testifying about why a situation, incident, or accident did or didn't occur as delineated in a complaint.

- Also remember that over 90 percent of all lawsuits settle before trial. However, once attorneys reach the point of deposing expert witnesses, the chances of them going to trial increase dramatically, so be prepared to go the distance.

The preceding information in this chapter provides some general information on what you can expect and what is expected of you if you're hired as an expert witness. Experts who are retained by attorneys follow some of the same rules when giving deposition testimony as other witnesses. However, there are some differences. For instance, expert witnesses are prohibited from testifying on matters that the average judge or juror should be familiar with. Therefore, a chemist called to testify about the characteristics of liquids when they boil can't say something like, "I think the babysitter was irresponsible because she should not have heated the baby's milk bottle so long in the microwave." Instead, they should say something to the effect of "In a 1200 watt microwave oven, liquids can reach their boiling point in less than a minute."

A common pitfall experts face is making the assumption that they can control the actual content of the information asked for because they have the specialized expertise that pertains to the matter being examined. Because they are credentialed, their opinions are valued, and often their lesser qualified peers may automatically follow their direction. Well, this same transference of authority isn't adhered to in the deposition process because what occurs during a deposition is governed by legal codes. I recall this happening when I reported a deposition during which a psychiatrist had been hired as an expert. He attempted to validated his response to a question by stating that he shouldn't be grilled so intently on whether or not a person's medication was sufficient because one could make the logical assumption that the doctor who prescribed the medicine would follow all the guidelines, because, after all, he's a well-respected specialist in the field. The examining attorney was quick to point out that when it comes to matters of law, "logic" is not the guiding principle. [Humm…..?] So when giving deposition testimony, expert witnesses have to be mindful of where they fit in the stratum of legal proceedings.

To be fair to the reader of this book, the rules of deposition testimony that govern expert witness testimony are more specific than they are for the layperson. For that reason, if you've been retained as an expert, and you're unfamiliar with giving expert deposition testimony, I suggest you go beyond this book and also review **Nolo's Deposition Handbook** by Attorneys Paul Bergman and Albert J. Moore. It has a broad section dedicated to expert witness testimony.

SUBSEQUENT EXAMINATIONS

After the examining attorney has concluded his initial examination, additional examinations may follow. These are usually shorter than the first examination, mainly because during the first examination all the foundational information that's needed is covered. Subsequent examinations may be by your attorney as he seeks to clarify some of the responses you gave. They may also be by other attorneys involved in the case who represent different clients (who may be lesser involved), and their questions will usually pertain more to the liability their particular client may have in the lawsuit. Many times right before the deposition concludes, your attorney may suggest a break be taken so as to find out from you, in a private discussion, if there's anything pertinent you feel he should ask you about that you didn't get a chance to talk about during the deposition. This way your attorney can ask his questions in an artful way to bring out a fact or event that may help your case. If an opposing attorney's client is present, their side may take a break for this same reason.

There may also be re-examinations, which means even though an attorney has already questioned you, following the questioning of another attorney he can reopen his examination and ask follow-up questions. As a rule, re-examinations tend to be brief.

—oOo—

COMING TO AN END

If the deposition is not completed, then it will be re-scheduled for another day. A deposition may not be finished in the time allotted for a number of reasons. Some of the usual ones are: time constraints on any of the key participants; because a witness (or one of the attorneys) did not bring requested documents that need to be examined; because the witness (or the court reporter) is tired. It's also not uncommon for the parties to listen to part of the evidence and then decide it's much more practical to attempt to settle the dispute rather than to continue on. So the deposition is adjourned, and settlement negotiations are begun.

If there is a subsequent session to a deposition because it had to be continued, the court reporter may not administer the oath again, but you are still under the initial oath you took to tell the truth. As a rule, continued depositions focus on additional information that's needed; they are not To go through ground already covered. If an attorney does stray into issues already gone over, one of the opposing attorneys will usually object as asked and answered.

As previously discussed, some time after the deposition process, the court reporter may prepare a transcript of the proceeding and will inform you (in writing) that the original transcript of your deposition testimony is completed and ready to be reviewed and signed. The time for doing this varies from jurisdiction to jurisdiction, but it's usually 30 days or less. If the transcript is not reviewed, then it's the usual practice for the parties on both side, and the Court, to consider whatever is contained in the transcript to be a true and accurate recording of what was said at the deposition (Also see pages 39-40).

Usually the deponent will go to the court reporter's office to review the deposition transcript. Oftentimes, though, if the witness' attorney has purchased a copy of the transcript, it's acceptable for the witness to review her attorney's copy and make the necessary changes. An advantage of doing it this way is an attorney can guide his client on making any changes she may choose to make. An attorney may also just send a copy to the witness.

The main thing reporters consider when they calculate the cost of a deposition transcript is how many pages the transcript contains. How much reporters charge for deposition transcripts varies widely, so it would not be helpful to put an estimated cost in this book. However, I will say that, overall, court reporters are well paid for their services. Another thing, in most jurisdictions, only parties to the lawsuit, or the attorneys representing them, are permitted to purchase a copy of the transcript from the court reporter.

Oftentimes attorneys stipulate that the court reporter can release the original copy of the transcript to an expert witness or professional witness such as a doctor. He/she can then review the original and return it to the court reporter. Court reporters tend to balk at this, and oftentimes have refused to do it because it requires them to release their work product, which can then be photocopied and passed around without them receiving payment for it.

Whether you review the original transcript or a copy, you are not to obliterate any of the text when making changes. Most reporters provide a transcript review sheet for this purpose, and this prevents witnesses from having to actually write on the transcript itself. Also, you can only change your answers, not any of the questions or other comments attorneys made.

If you gave deposition testimony because you were subpoenaed to do so, you are entitled to a witness fee and possibly reimbursement for travel expenses. The attorney who subpoenaed you is legally obligated to compensate you. The amount of this compensation for giving a deposition is governed by code sections; however, even to this exceptions have been made. I'm reminded of the employee who worked for a fast food restaurant (probably for minimum wage). She was subpoenaed to testify about an accident she witnessed at the restaurant. The deposition was set on her day off so it wouldn't interfere with her being unavailable at her workstation. She sent the attorneys a message by her boss, telling them she didn't have money to pay a babysitter, so she would have to bring her baby and preschooler with her. The attorneys, four in all, chipped in to cover the cost of her sitter. One of them commented "We did it because attorneys are such nice guys." [Hum.......?]

SAMPLE TRANSCRIPTS

Transcript I

The transcript that follows contains excerpts from testimony taken at an actual deposition. The witness' responses to the questions demonstrate her ability to provide answers that strengthen her position. Some of the factors that show her skill in answering questions are: if she wasn't answering the exact question that was asked, she made this clear in her answer; if she didn't understand a question, she said so; if she needed to explain or clarify her answer, she did so; if she didn't know the answer to a question, many times she would state why she didn't know; if she was asked about the contents of a document and needed to see the document before answering a question, she asked to see it; if there was an opportunity for her to include in her answer information that might be damaging to the credibility of the other side, she did that; she did not allow herself to be misquoted; if she needed a recess to talk to her attorney, she requested one. In essence, she wasn't intimidated by the questioning attorney.

At the same time, though, her interjections were not so intrusive, or outlandish, as to be characterized as being obstructive to the process. She didn't cross that line, and I suggest that you don't either.

A Word of Caution

This transcript has been included to demonstrate how a witness can answer questions effectively; however this witness is a plaintiff. Plaintiffs' answers tend to be wordy because they're attempting to get their complaints out. If you are a defendant in a lawsuit, it's advisable that you answer questions more concisely so as to not open up additional areas to be questioned about. Witnesses who are not a party to the lawsuit, that have no personal interest in its outcome, do not have to be as much concerned about answering questions strategically. Expert witnesses also tend to give wordy answers because they have been hired to give their professional opinions about the matters the lawsuit involves. They are also attempting to build the case of the attorney who hired them, so their answers are expected to be wordy.

Deposition Transcript

BE IT REMEMBERED that, pursuant to Notice, and on Friday, the 27th day of September, 2002, commencing at the hour of 10:00 in the morning thereof, at the Law Offices of Farnsworth, Crowley & Zibbits, 1481 Lake Park Drive, suite 2201, Vacaville, California, before me, VERONICA CURRY, a duly Certified Shorthand Reporter, in and for the County of Sacramento, State of California, there personally appeared

ANGELA M. LATHAN

Called as a witness by the Defendant, who, being by me first duly sworn, was thereupon examined and testified as follows:

EXAMINATION BY MS. ZIBBITS

Q   Good morning, ma'am.

My name is Aretha Zibbits, and I'm the attorney representing ScanVech in the complaint you filed against them.

A   Good morning.

Q   State your full name for the record, please.

A   Angela M. Lathan.

Q   Where do you live, Angela—may I call you "Angela"?

A   That's fine.

In Modesto, 1111 Amber Lane.

Q   Angela, have you ever had your deposition taken before?

A   In this matter?

Q   In any matter.

A   Yes.

Q   How many times?

A   I believe twice.

Q   Did these two times involve a lawsuit where you were suing somebody, or were you being sued?

A   Neither. Both times involved me being a witness at my former place of employment.

Q   Where was that?

A   The depositions or my place of employment?

Q   Your place of employment.

A   Riverside Learning Academy in Houston.

Q   Do you remember the name of the law firm that represented your side in the matter?

A   As I said, I was not a party to the action.

Q   Sorry. I mean who represented your employer?

A   Not off the top of my head I don't remember.

Q   Do you have any written information that would contain that information?

A   I may have kept a copy of the subpoenas I was sent, but I'm not for sure.

MS. ZIBBITS: Laurice, I'd like to have that information. When she gets it to you, you can just pass it on to me.

MS. BAUER: Sure

THE WITNESS: Excuse me, but I need to say something to my attorney.

MS. BAUER: Give us a moment, Aretha.

(Discussion off the record between
the deponent and her attorney)

MS. BAUER: Okay, Aretha, but my client just wants me to remind you that she said she "may" have a copy. She's not certain she does.

MS. ZIBBITS: Understood. If she has the information, I would like it.

Q   BY MS. ZIBBITS: Let me go over a couple of things. First of all, you've been sworn today, and you'll be giving your testimony under oath, the same as if you were testifying in a courtroom. And it places upon you the same obligation to answer questions truthfully and accurately to the best of your ability. Do you understand that?

A   Yes.

Q   If throughout the deposition I ask you a question you don't understand, please just tell me you don't understand it, and I'll try to rephrase it so you do understand.

A   Okay.

Q   If I ask you a question and you don't hear part of it, let me know you haven't heard it, and I'll repeat it or ask the court reporter to read it back to you.

A   Sure.

Q   If I ask you a question and you don't know the answer, it's okay to say you don't know.

A   Yes.

Q   I don't want you to guess or speculate. If I ask a question and the only way you can answer it is by guessing, I'd rather you tell me that. I may re-ask the question, but instead I'll ask you for your best estimate, and we'll know it's not an exact answer. I'm entitled to have the best estimate you can give me.

A   Yes.

Q   If at any time during the deposition you need to take a break, that's fine. This is not an endurance contest. Just tell me you need to take a break. If there's a question pending, I'll probably ask you to answer that question before breaking.

A   Okay.

Q   To assist the court reporter, it's important for all your responses to be in words, "yes or no," or some other words. Although in everyday speech it's common to shake or nod your head or say "uh-huh" or "uhn-uhn," or even grunt sometimes, those types of responses don't come out well in the deposition transcript, and too often when we see those types of responses, attorneys have to guess at what was really meant.

Also, it's important for only one of us to speak at a time because as talented as our reporter is, she still can only take down one person talking at a time.

A   All right.

Q   So let me finish my complete question before you start answering, and I'll let you finish your answer before I ask another question.

A   All right.

Q   Frequently my questions are so simple, by the time I get halfway through you'll know what I'm asking, and you'll want to give an answer before I get the question out. This happens all the time in ordinary conversation. But if it happens here, I'll remind you to wait.

A   I'll try not to do that.

Q   Do you have any questions before we go on?

A   No, I don't.

Q   Oh, I almost forgot. Once the deposition is transcribed and put in a booklet form, you'll have the opportunity to review it and make changes. I caution you, though, if you change an answer during your review and it contradicts the testimony you give during the deposition, I'll have the opportunity to point that out to a judge or jury if this case goes to trial. And my doing so could affect you credibility.

Do you understand that?

A   I do. But let me inform you, if I discover a mistake—and I don't care who made it, me or the court reporter—most likely I will correct it.

Q   That's your right to do so. Let's move on.

Are you employed?

A   Not currently.

Q   What was the last job you held?

A   The job at ScanVech, the one this lawsuit is about.

Q   I see. What position did you hold at ScanVech?

A   At the time I was let go, office manager.

Q   What was your last day of employment there?

A   Well, I was on the payroll until January 15, 2002.

Q   Oh, I mean the last day you actually worked?

A   I can't remember exactly. I think it was sometime in November of 2001, the week before Thanksgiving seems right. It's in my records that I brought with me today.

Q   Why did you leave?

A   I was unfairly terminated.

Q   Were you given a notice—

A   Yes—

Q   Let me finish the question.

A   I'm sorry, I thought you were done.

Q   Were you given a notice informing you when your last day of work would be?

A   Yes, a verbal one.

Q   When?

A   The day I was let go.

MS. ZIBBITS: Before we began, I had the reporter mark a series of documents as exhibits. I'll now show the Witness what was marked Deposition Exhibit A for identification.

Q   BY MS. ZIBBITS: Angela, Deposition Exhibit A is a letter to you from a Miss Owens, dated September 1, 1998. It's on ScanVech letterhead. It's informing you that as of November 20th, 2001, your services will no longer be needed at ScanVech due to the ending of the state contract.

Have you seen this document before?

A   No, I've never seen this document before.

Q   Well, it's addressed to you, and there's a place where you signed it to acknowledge receipt of it.

A   Well, the document is falsified.

Q   Are you saying you believe it's falsified?

A   I'm saying I know that's a falsified document.

Q   It has your signature on it.

A   Yes, but it's also the original, and if I would have received it, I would have the original in my personal file, not ScanVech.

Q   What, if anything, else leads you to say it's falsified?

A   Like I said, I only received verbal notification that my services were no longer needed, and that came sometime in November. Also, on the signature of this document, there's no middle initial in my name. I always use my middle initial when I sign my name, so I know I didn't sign that.

Q   So you don't recall receiving any letter or memo that had the information that Exhibit A contains?

A   No, I don't recall. I don't recall because I never received any written notification.

Q   Now, I'd like to refer you to Deposition Exhibit B, a document you produced, which is a memo to Miss Owens from you, regarding a new position opening up for an onsite coordinator of the information system upgrade. The first sentence in paragraph three says: "Although I would very much like to fill the position of onsite coordinator, it is only a 50 percent time position, and it would not adequately fulfill my salary requirements."

Do you recall having a discussion with Miss Owens about appointing you to that position?

A   I don't recall a discussion about that, but I recall the position.

Q   Was that position offered to you?

A   Yes.

Q   And you don't recall the discussion that you had with Miss Owens, whereby she stated that while the position is currently only 50 percent time that once the money from the Sacramento Foundation was received that the position would be turned into a full-time position, and the salary for it would surpass your present salary?

A   No, no such discussion ever took place. Besides, the money that was allotted for the position was supposed to come entirely from a government contract. The Sacramento Foundation does not provide funds for administrative positions such as that.

Q   How do you know that they don't?

A   Because my position as the office manager required me to be familiar with what funds were available for the different needs the company had.

Q   Wasn't the comptroller at ScanVech the person that you were to go to with technical questions about what was permissible and not permissible regarding financial matters that you encountered as the office manager at ScanVech?

A   Only for accounting questions that related directly to financial matters, not when it came to identifying what a funder specified their monies should be used for.

Q   I'd now like to refer you to a document that's been marked Exhibit C. It's a memo to you. I direct your attention to where it says "from J.P. Owens, associate director." Do you recognize those initials as being Miss Owens'?

A   I have a very bad copy here.

Q   Is it too bad for you to recognize the handwriting?

A   Yes.

Q   Okay, I'll dig out the original.

(Pause in proceedings)

I'm now showing you the original of the memo.

A   Okay, I now recognize the initials, but I also have another comment to make regarding this memorandum.

Q   Which memorandum?

A   This memo you just showed me, Exhibit C.

And I would comment, based on your production of the original, that this is another document I never received.

Q   Because I have the original?

A   Yes.

Q   You don't know where it came from, do you?

A   No, but it certainly didn't come to me, or I would have it. So I think—

Q   You've answered the question.

A   Excuse me.

Q   So you're saying you've never received this memo before, a copy of it?

A   Neither a copy nor the original.

Q   Isn't it true that it would have been in your personnel file?

A   Not if it was supposed to be received by me. Maybe a copy of it after I reviewed it and signed off saying I received it.

Q   So you don't believe you placed it in your personnel file?

A   I certainly did not.

And I don't believe it should have been part of my file, as per the personnel policy and procedures.

Q   What part of the policy do you believe impacts on Exhibit C?

A   If you give me a copy of the policy, I'll show it to you.

(Counsel passes the Witness a document to review)

It's in paragraph 2A, under "Operating Procedures."

Q   Oh, I see it. All right.

Now I show you a copy of Deposition exhibit D, which is a memo that bears the date of June 1, 2001. Do you have any reason to believe this document was not written on the 1st of June.

A   I would not know if it was or wasn't.

Q   Has anyone told you that this document was written at any time other than the 1st of June 2001?

A   No one has discussed this memorandum with me, the date of it or anything else about it.

Q   Angela, you are aware that Anna Welsh filed a written grievance regarding an incident between you and her; is that correct?

A   I need some clarification. It's my impression that the grievance was regarding the incident relating to her, not an incident between her and me.

Q   Explain the incident as you recall it?

A   Basically, it was her objection to my presenting her to the board as an employee who was dissatisfied with her salary. Even though she had told me she was dissatisfied.

Q   What did you tell the board about her salary?

A   I don't recall verbatim what I said to them, but the crux of it was that she was dissatisfied she wasn't being paid what the salary scale allowed for that position, and she had indicated some annoyance about that to me.

Q   Anything else that you can remember?

A   To be specific, she was also annoyed because the

other field assistant, Beverly Valerian, who was hired some months after Anna, was on a higher salary scale than she. And also—

Q   Is the difference between what Beverly and Anna was making all you discussed with the board?

A   I started to state—before you interrupted me—I believe the discussion was more than about just the difference between Anna's and Beverly's salaries. Anna was even more concerned that she was not being paid what her predecessor, Marva Reynolds, had been paid.

Q   Do you know what the difference was between Anna's and Beverly's salaries?

A   Not without looking at the payroll sheets, no.

Q   How much higher was one than the other?

A   The only way I can answer that is by looking at the payroll sheet.

Q   I'm asking from your own personal memory.

A   That is not something I retained in my memory, so I am unable to answer the question.

Q   Other than the fact that she was on a different salary scale, what else did Anna complain about?

A   At this moment I don't recall other specifics.

Q   But there were other complaints?

A   Yes. And if they come to me later during this deposition, I'll let you know.

Q   I'm now showing you a document that has previously been marked Deposition Exhibit E. It's another document that you indicated was erroneous. What about that document do you believe is inaccurate?

A   In paragraph five, Miss Owens indicates I approached her with unsolicited information about things the staff was saying about her ability to supervise. And it's my recollection that she came to me with her own information, with her own questions in mind. So the emphasis on saying I approached her is not correct.

Q   Now I show you a document previously marked Deposition Exhibit F, which is Anna Welsh's grievance of July 2, 2001. Is there anything contained in this document that you believe is incorrect or untrue.

A   I think that my statements to the board, as noted in paragraph two of this document, were not statements that necessarily cast a bad light on Miss Welsh, as indicated, but rather they were intended to clarify some things.

Q   Before you went to the board and made any statements concerning her dissatisfaction with circumstances surrounding her salary, did you tell Anna Welsh that you intended to go to the board with that information?

A   I didn't discuss that with her, no.

Q   She didn't authorize you to do that, though, did she?

A   No, but I did not need her authorization to discuss issues with the board.

Q   Did Anna Welsh come to you in confidence when she expressed her dissatisfaction?

A   The conversations that she had with me were in my office.

Q   But were they in confidence?

A   They were not represented to me as being confidential or strictly between her and me. They were discrete in that no one else was present, but I never was told that information was confidential enough that it should never be shared with another individual.

Q   Now, when Anna Welsh made her grievance, did she follow the organization's grievance procedure?

MS. BAUER: Which grievance, counsel, the formal or informal?

MS. ZIBBITS: The one under the grievance procedure of the policy manual at ScanVech.

MS. BAUER: There are two types indicated. One is informal, and the other is a written grievance.

MS. ZIBBITS: Are you testifying, counsel?

MS. BAUER: No, but your question is vague and ambiguous, and I instruct her not to answer it as phrased.

Q   BY MS. ZIBBITS: Do you differentiate between "formal" versus "informal" grievance procedures?

A   Yes.

Q   Do you believe, as your attorney represented a few moments ago, that there's more than one grievance procedure at ScanVech?

A   I would ask to be able to review the personnel manual's section on grievances before answering that.

Q   Since you don't know from your own personal knowledge, we'll move on.

Now, you had a conversation with Anna Welsh before the board meeting. What did she say to you initially?

A   The conversation immediately preceding the meeting?

Q   Yes.

A   There was almost no communication between us that day. But what I can remember is I passed by her desk and asked her if she was aware of the subject to be discussed at the meeting. And she said "Yes"—with a huge sigh. I commented to her that she didn't seem to be too happy about being able to clear the air, and she said she wasn't. But at the same time she said she would be happy if it resulted in her receiving a more equitable salary.

Q   Anna talked about her salary to you at that time?

A   Just the statement that I just told you.

Q   Now, do you recall her saying in the grievance meeting that she was very upset about your going to the board on her behalf?

A   First I need to clarify the question. I was not speaking on her behalf. I was speaking on a number of items. I was not trying to rescue her from any particular situation. I was citing a list of wrongs I saw at ScanVech. I did not intend to correct her situation specifically.

But yes, she did say she was upset because I went to the board.

Q   So in your opinion, you told the board about Anna

because of a complaint you had about Miss Owens, the associate director?

A   More specifically, a complaint I had about Miss Owens's management practices.

Q   Now, as a result of issues you raised at the board meeting, a grievance meeting was subsequently held, August 24th, 2001. Do you recall that?

A   Yes.

Q   What time did you leave the office after the grievance meeting?

A   At the end of the workday, around 5:00.

Q   Do you recall how the matter was left at the end of the grievance meeting?

A   I didn't feel there was a conclusion to the issues because there was no definitive next step. There was a conclusion to the meeting, but not to the issue.

Q   Do you believe the meeting held for addressing the grievance was formal or informal?

A   I believe it was formal.

Q   What about the meeting leads you to believe it was formal?

A   I would say the very nature, the way it was handled. The fact that a memo had been put out by Miss Owens, requiring that Anna Welsh and I both be there.

Q   What do you mean by "the very nature"?

A   I felt very, very strongly I was being accused of causing a ruckus in the office. I didn't feel there was an open discussion or an agenda for my responses. Miss Owens started off saying the discussion was supposed to be informal and courteous, and I think that we deviated from that platform early on.

Q   What about the meeting was not courteous?

A   My recollection is that Miss Owens was very adamant—when Miss Owens felt that I was asking Anna too many questions about why the memo was written and who had urged me to write it, Miss Owens' demeanor was very abrupt and angry. She said stuff like, "It's my job to run this company, not yours, Miss Lathan. Where do you get off writing a memo to the board. You're just the office manager, and that means you just run the operations in the office, and you're not in charge of managing this company."

As I continued to question Anna, so as to get to the crux of our differences, Miss Owens kept saying,

"Miss Welsh is not the one being accused here, Miss Lathan." And that led me to believe that I was the one being accused.

Q   What else about Miss Owens' behavior led you to believe that this was not an informal meeting?

A   The fact that I had worked beside her for about four and a half years, and I could tell when she was being informal and when she was being formal, her tone. I could also tell from her process, from her demeanor, how she approached the topic. She had the meeting tape recorded. She called us by our last names rather than our first names as she normally does.

Q   At the meeting, what procedure was used for processing the grievance?

A   In my opinion, we never utilized a procedure all throughout, therefore I can't answer your question. I never witnessed a laid-out procedure. It was a shouting match. I'm sure if you review the tape recording of it, you can tell that.

Q   Do you recall making the statement in the grievance meeting in Miss Owens' office, "Are you having memory lapses?" Did you make that statement to Miss

Owens?

A   No, I did not. Wait a minute, I would like to change that. I may have made that remark. Taken out of context, it sounds strange, but I believe I may have said that.

Q   What was the context of the statement?

A   Miss Owens prided herself on having total recall, and I believe there was something that she had done or written within a short period of time, perhaps even in the meeting itself, that she had forgotten about. So I may have made that comment to that occurrence.

Q   I believe you already testified that you left the office the day of the meeting at 5:00. Do you recall testifying to that earlier?

A   I recall the question, but I don't recall exactly how I answered.

MS. ZIBBITS: Miss Reporter, will you read back that question and answer, please.

(The record was read back.)

THE WITNESS: That refreshed my memory. I do recall answering that.

Q   BY MS. ZIBBITS: Isn't it true you were at Scan-Vech's offices for only about 35 minutes on November 20th, the last day you actually showed up to work at ScanVech?

A   I may have been there approximately 35 minutes.

Q   Do you recall checking your mailbox to see if you had any memos or other mail in the box, before you left the office that day?

A   I don't recall either way, whether I did or didn't.

Q   I'm going to backtrack a minute, back to the conversations you had with Anna before the grievance meeting.

Do you recall from the conversation that you had with Anna, about this purported dissatisfaction, what, if anything, she was going to do about it?

A   I'm not sure if I understand your question. Please rephrase it.

Q   Was there any action to be taken that you discussed, action by you or Anna to resolve her dissatisfaction?

A   I don't recall anything specific.

Q   Do you recall anything in general?

THE WITNESS: Sharon, may I speak with you for a minute.

MS. BAUER: Sure.

Aretha, we'll take a break for a minute.

As a matter of fact, we've been going for awhile. I'm sure

the court reporter could use a break also. Let's make it a little longer one.

(A recess was taken.)

MS. ZIBBITS: Angela, you didn't answer my last question. Do you need it read back?

THE WITNESS: Yes, that would be helpful.

(The record was read back.)

The answer to the question is no, I don't recall anything in general.

Q   BY MS. ZIBBITS: So did you view these conversations with Anna Welsh as just sort of general complaining about a situation?

A   No, I regarded them as specific complaints about a situation. And at that point I had already directed a number of comments to the board regarding a number of other issues regarding the situation with Miss Owens.

Q   Now, let's review your memorandum, Exhibit G, wherein you stated, "I commented to Anna that such change would only be official if approved by the board of directors, and no such approval had been recorded."

Does that refresh your recollection that you actually told her that the board had to approve changes in classification and rate of pay?

A   To be honest with you, I don't recall if it was my comment that initially informed her of that or whether it was her reading of the personnel manual that first informed her of that.

Q   Now, in paragraph 7 you state that you told Anna Welsh that her predecessor, Marva Reynolds, left ScanVech because she was at the top of the salary scale for that position and had been offered a job elsewhere that provided greater earning and growth potential.

        Is that the only reason you gave as to why that former employee left ScanVech?

A   At the time, yes.

Q   Did you tell Anna anything else about that later?

A   I don't recall. I may have.

Q   What do you think you told Anna Welsh at a later date about the reason that Marva Reynolds left ScanVech?

A   I may have informed her that Miss Reynolds was no longer happy at ScanVech because due to working with Miss Owens, she was feeling frazzled and was looking to get out.

Q   Isn't it true you encouraged Miss Reynolds to take the job that she eventually took?

A   Miss Reynolds told me about the job, but I did not encourage her to take that or any job, specifically. She informed me she went on the interview and liked the job. She said she liked the salary. She decided on her own to go for it. I told her it sounded like an excellent opportunity, but I did not encourage her to take that job versus any other position.

Q   Did you have any discussions with her about taking that job?

A   As I just said, she told me about it, so obviously we had a discussion about her taking the job. But again, I didn't urge her to take it.

Q   Now, you talked to an auditor for the federal government, a Mr. Wazniky, about some of your concerns at Scan-Vech. Do you recall what you talked to him about?

A   Specifically, no, but the primary focus was the federal contracts.

Q   What about the federal contracts?

A   The methods ScanVech used to modify the federal contracts.

Q   What led to the discussion about the modifications in the federal contracts?

A   When I contacted them, how Miss Owens had modified the federal contracts was my main concern. And I don't think they would have come all the way to the West coast if they weren't seriously concerned about those modifications.

MS. ZIBBITS: I move to strike the last part of the witness' answer as nonresponsive, starting with "And I don't think."

Q   BY MS. ZIBBITS: Do you know if the auditors found any improprieties in the federal contracts?

A   I have not been made privy to their findings.

Q   So you don't know?

A   No. But I certainly would like to know.

Q   Did anybody else meet with you and the auditors?

A   Not simultaneously. They met with me and other people, but not with us jointly.

Q   Did you only have one meeting with the auditors?

A   No, there were two.

Q   When was the second meeting?

A   I believe it was on or about the day that they got a court order, from a judge here in California, to commence the audit.

Q   What court order is that?

A   I don't know. They just mentioned they had to have a

judge's order to enter the premises and secure documentation.

Q   Isn't that how they routinely obtain entrance to premises to conduct an audit?

A   I have no idea what they routinely do. You'll have to ask them.

Q   Just answer the question, please. All of your add-ons in your answers are unnecessary.

A   I can see why you'd say that. But I will try to do better.

Q   Before you contacted the auditors during November of last year, did you call any of the board members to find out what, if anything, had been done by them to look more closely at the day-to-day operations at ScanVech?

A   I don't recall that I called them. I know I wrote them. Those letters and memorandums are part of the paperwork that I supplied you with.

Q   The question is whether you called any board members sometime in, or before, November of last year?

A   I responded that I don't recall whether I called them.

MS. ZIBBITS: Let me check my notes. I think I'm about done. Yes, I am.

Thank you very much, Miss Angela.

MS. BAUER: Before we end, I have a few follow-up questions.

EXAMINATION BY MS. BAUER

Q   Angela, was it required under ScanVech's contract with the Department of Information that the associate director's time sheets and expense reimbursement forms be reviewed by someone else other than the associate director herself?

A   Yes.

Q   Where is that instruction found?

A   It was information I gleaned from part of a training seminar, given by the state, that I attended in September of 2000. It was part of the state's operating guidelines for agencies that received government funds.

Q   And by having these billings verified, did that make it easier for the state contracting agency to verify that all billings submitted for payment were accurate and honest?

MS. ZIBBITS: Objection, leading, asks for information beyond this witness' knowledge. Outside the scope of my direct.

Go ahead.

MS. BAUER: I'll rephrase the question.

Q   BY MS. BAUER: Why do you believe the state required that someone other than herself review the associate director's time sheets and expense reimbursement forms.

A   To prevent improprieties relating to misuse of funds, like the improprieties I've brought out in this deposition.

MS. BAUER: Thank you. Nothing further.

MS. ZIBBITS: I need to follow up on your last line of questioning for just a minute.

EXAMINATION BY MS. ZIBBITS

Q   The improprieties you are talking about, you're basing them upon your own perception, right, because you don't know the results of the audit of ScanVech?

A   Yes, but my perception is also based—

Q   You've answered the question.

MS. BAUER: Counsel, you need to allow her to finish her answer. If it turns out to be nonresponsive, it can always be stricken.

Go ahead, Angela.

THE WITNESS: My perception of what was improper is based on what I encountered in my job responsibilities. I was directly in charge of counting the employees' hours up based on their time sheets. I also had access to copies of the expense vouchers. And I knew what the state guidelines were.

MS. ZIBBITS: Thank you. Nothing further.

MS. BAUER: That's it.

(The deposition concluded at 12:00 p.m.)

_____

Angela M. Lathan

_____

Date Signed

—oOo—

Transcript II

Now that you've been made aware of some of the steps deponents can take to increase their chances of giving deposition testimony they feel good about and is in their best interests, we'll look at one of the main ways deponents go astray when testifying: ***volunteering too much information***. This pitfall would happen less often if deponents were made aware of it before the start of a deposition. An attorney's advisement might be worded like this: *Just answer what is asked; don't volunteer additional information; generally, the shorter your answers the better.* When deponents deviate from this caution unnecessarily—or unknowingly—the proceedings can take an unneeded turn and an opposing attorney can then probe into additional areas surrounding their affairs.

        The paragraphs that follow are taken from another publication by this author," The Deposition Handbook Addendum or How People Mess Up During Depositions." That guide was written to give people a sample of how deposition questioning goes and also to point out how a deponent can open up a whole new line of questioning by volunteering information that's not asked for. The questions contained in the Addendum's sample transcript were detailed, and the questioning attorney was thorough in her examination, but the deponent still should have been more mindful about strictly answering the question asked. Take for example this excerpt from page 113:

Q   **...Are you presently employed?**

A   **Yes, I'm a cosmetologist, got my license six**

months ago. Since I got out of that marriage, I'm now much more productive.

Q   I see. So you're now able to earn a living wage?

A   Uhhh, yes.

There was no need for the deponent to volunteer that she got her cosmetology license or that she's much more productive. The simple answer to "Are you presently employed?" should have been "yes." Let the opposing counsel fish for additional information because oftentimes they won't, and that can be to your advantage. Although the caution about being too wordy applies to almost all kinds of deposition proceedings, for the deponent in Sample Transcript II, who's involved in a dissolution of marriage and property settlement dispute, providing that type of additional information can be particularly damaging.

Of course, this witness's attorney could have (and probably should have) objected that the witness's answers were outside the scope and asked that the answers be stricken. But all attorneys aren't created equally. Some are better trained and more cognizant, so they are better able to look out for their clients' rights than others are.

Sample Transcript II is riddled with other examples of the deponent divulging too much information. Each example of this is shown in bold type to make it easy for you to examine the occurrences. Because of the extraneous information that was volunteered, the testimony concludes with the examining attorney stating she'll need additional time to conduct the deposition. This is one of the things that make legal proceedings drag out, and it also adds considerably to attorney costs and fees—not to mention the infringement on a party's own time. The way the proceedings that follow unfold is something that most people want to avoid.

BE IT REMEMBERED that pursuant to Notice, and on Tuesday, the 6th day of March, 2007, commencing a the hour of 10:00 a.m. in the morning thereof, at the Law Offices of Bessel, Franks & Tressford, 1389 W. 3000th Street, Chicago, Illinois, before me, SANDLE HINESON, a duly Certified Shorthand Reporter, in and for the County of Cook, Chicago, Illinois there personally appeared

TREFANIE M. ROOKTON

called as a witness by the Respondent, who, being by me first duly sworn, was examined and testified as follows:

EXAMINATION BY MS. TRESSFORD

Q   What is your home address?

A   888 Blossom Boulevard, Chicago, Illinois, 60688

Q   Do you own that home?

A   Yes, I do.

Q   But you're still paying a mortgage, right?

A   Oh, yes, I am.

Q   How is title held to that house?

A   Under my name and my ex-husband's name.

Q   What is your monthly mortgage payment?

A $1880.34.

Q   Do you know how much of that mortgage pay-ment per year is applied to the interest on your residence?

A   I would have to look that up.

Q   Would that amount be set forth in your income tax return for last year?

A   I'm pretty sure it would.

Q   During your marriage, did you have any income from work that you did?

A   No, I didn't work. **I was a married woman, so the way I look at it, he was supposed to work and pay the bills.**

Q   I see.

Are you presently employed?

A   **Yes, I'm a cosmetologist, got my license six months ago. Since I got out of that marriage, I'm now much more productive.**

Q   **I see. So you're now able to earn a living wage?**

A.   **Uhhh, yes.**

Q   And you and Mr. Junkins file a joint income tax return?

A   Yes. **And we got a refund for the past five years. That's how I was able to take the trip to Paris, in case you're wondering.**

Q   I see. Did Mr. Junkins, your ex-husband, travel to

Paris with you?

A   No.

Q   Do you have a copy of your last year's tax return?

A   Yes, but not with me today.

Q   By the end of next week, will you give a copy of your tax return for last year to Ms. Hillsmith, your attorney?

A   Yes.

MS. TRESSFORD: After you get that return, will you send a copy to my office?

MS. HILLSMITH: Sure.

Q   BY MS. TRESSFORD: Do you know what the fair market value of your home is?

A   I believe it's about five hundred.

Q   Five hundred what?

A   Oh, five hundred thousand.

Q   How much did you purchase it for?

A   Five hundred thirty thousand.

Q   Was the home recently appraised for that amount, or is that $500,000 just an estimate on your part?

A   No, it was appraised.

Q   By whom?

A   A real estate agent from Soxen and Yapper Realty. **Actually, He wasn't a licensed appraiser. He just sold houses.**

Q   So that appraisal wasn't done by a certified real estate appraiser; it's only a comparable done by a real estate sales agent?

A   Yes.

Q   Yes what?

A   Yes, it's a comparable.

Q   Did you put a down payment on that home?

A   Yes, I did.

Q   How much was the down payment?

A   I don't remember. **I know my dad lent me some money.**

Q   Did you repay your dad?

A   **Mr. Junkins and I were in the process of repaying him before he slipped into the coma, after his accident?**

Q   Does your dad have a conservator?

A   Yes, I'm the conservator, **but I'm not court-appointed. I just take care of his business.**

Q   Let me get this straight. You take care of your

dad's business affairs, but you're not court-appointed?

A   Right, I just do it.

Q   Is that agreement in writing, the agreement regarding the terms of your repaying him for the money he lent you to purchase your house?

A   Yes, it is, but I don't have a copy of it. My only copy was destroyed **when my home was flooded last year.**

Q   Oh, so the house that you and Mr. Junkins own was flooded?

A   Yes.

Q   Did you receive any compensation from your insurance company for flood damage that was done to the home?

A   Yes, around $40,000, **but Mr. Junkins did most of the repairs.**

Q   Um, $40,000. And you said Mr. Junkins did most of the repairs.

Well, the flood occurred before Mr. Junkins moved away from the house, right?

A   Yes.

Q   How much of that $40,000 did you give to your

former husband, Mr. Junkins, my client?

A   Nothing.   **I was so upset with him that I didn't think he was entitled to anything.**

Q   Let me be clear. This flood occurred while he was still living with you in the family home?

A   Yes.

Q   You telling me about the flood and the insurance settlement opens up another area of questioning.

MS. TRESSFORD: Miss Hillsmith, it looks to me like we should continue this deposition to another date. I want to subpoena from the insurance company the records regarding the flood settlement. I also want to examine their income tax returns for the last few years. And I need to examine any written documents showing how payments were made to her father for the money he lent her for a down payment on the house. We weren't privy to any of this information prior to this deposition, and receiving it now has opened up new areas of questioning.

Q   BY MS. TRESSFORD: How many years of previous tax returns do you have?

A   I don't know, about three.

Q   When we continue the deposition, make sure you've turned any of those returns over to your attorney. And also turn over to her written information you may have about the insurance reimbursement for the flooding of the house. And, as previously mentioned, anything that relates to the repayment of the money that your father lent you for the purchase of your house.

Just so you'll know, I do expect the next session of this deposition to be longer, so be prepared to spend more time here.

MS. TRESSFORD: Is that okay with you, Counsel?

MS. HILLSMITH: That's fine.

MS. TRESSFORD: So we'll adjourn until a future date to be set by counsel.

_____

Trefanie M. Rookton

_____

Date Signed

—oOo—

OTHER USEFUL RESOURCES

Your attorney should be the first person you turn to for the information you need, but sometimes he may not be available or he may even charge you for his time when he has to communicate with you on the phone or by email. So it's good to know there are other places you can turn to for general information. One of the main places is a law library. The main courthouse of every county has a legal library that is available for public use, and librarians are available there to help guide you to specific topics. Many colleges and universities also have legal libraries. Also, the clerk of the court where your case is filed is one of the best sources to check with when trying to find out what local requirements apply to cases in specific jurisdictions. You can ask the clerk of the court for copies of any local discovery and deposition rules, and usually you'll only have to pay whatever the county charges for making copies.

What follows here are some internet sites where you can go to get additional information about the law and some more or less specific answers to questions about the type of case you're involved in.

- **Federal Rules of Civil Procedure — www.law.cornell. edu/rules**. This site contains the rules that govern the conduct of all civil actions brought in federal district courts. While they don't apply to lawsuits in state courts, the rules of many states are closely patterned on the federal rules. However, in legal proceedings, judges attempt to make rulings that follow the law to the letter, and state and local rules often take precedence over federal rules, so be sure to familiarize yourself with them.

- **National Center for State Courts** — **www.ncsconline. org/**. Links to the individual state court pages, for all 50 states, can be found on this site. It also has a page titled "Self-Representation Court Forms State Links" where you can actually view and copy the forms used in the court for your specific state.

- **Lawyers.Com** — **www.lawyers.com**. This site has message boards, which are separated by legal category and are monitored by attorneys and other legal professionals. Post a question and oftentimes you get a number of on-target responses. And you're free to ask for additional informational about the replies you receive. They have easy-to-understand legal articles that pertain to different aspects of the law. They have web discussions at various times on various topics, and they have an attorney data base, which can be useful if you're trying to hire an attorney. There's no charge for posting your questions or reading their legal articles.

- **A Good Lawyer** — **www.agoodlawyer.com** — This is a site that features a very short book (same name as the site) by Stephen W. Comiskey, written for lawyers that helps them deal with ethical considerations that may arise in how they handle their clients' cases. If you have questions about whether your attorney is handling your case in an ethical way, this is a good site to check out.

- **Findlaw.Com** — **www.findlaw.com**. This site was listed as one of **"Time"** news magazine's 50 Coolest Websites. The "For the Public" section contains a truck-load of information and resources on everything from living wills to bankruptcy to divorce, etc. Other areas are

designed for students, businesses, and legal professionals. It's well organized and extremely useful. To be listed
as one of **"Time's"** top 50 says a lot when it's in compe-
tition with thousands of other legal sites on the web. The
main reason it's included here is it's a legal site that links
to the actual case citations governing legal issues. Also,
one of its pages is **"Low or No-cost Legal Assistance"** — **http://www.findlaw.com/14firms/legalaid.
html**.

- **Ashcraft and Gerel.com** — **www.ashcraftandgerel.
com/links.html#medicalrecords**. This site links to a
rather large listing of medical sites, so if your case involves an injury, this is a great resource to use for possibly getting answers to any questions you may have
about it as it pertains to your case.

- **Mediate.com** — **www.mediate.com**. Here you can find
specific information on how mediation works. This information is extremely useful because the vast majority of
all lawsuits never go to trial. They're settled outside of
court. In fact, judges have been known to get upset with
attorneys who don't work hard enough to get their clients
to settle their lawsuits before trial. Even when court-
rooms are being assigned, civil trials are always secon-
dary to criminal cases when the priority of these assign-
ments are set, so understanding the mediation process
can be very useful to you.

- If you're convinced you want to go through the deposition process, and your entire case, without an attorney
(pro se or pro per) then check out **Nolo's site, www.nolo.
com**. They have a wide selection of self-help books and
software that can make do-it-yourself law easier. In fact,

they too have a deposition handbook (*Nolo's Deposition Handbook* by Paul Bergman and Albert J. Moore), which is excellent. However, it's also more voluminous than this book, so it gives you much more information to have to wade through. This book (the book you're now reading) gives you the basics, what's essential to know to help you feel empowered during the deposition procedure. Because Nolo's book is more voluminous, if you don't allow yourself adequate time to review it, you could end up feeling less prepared when you step into a deposition. However, it is well indexed, making it somewhat easier to find specific topics.

- **Self Help Support** — **http://selfhelpsupport.org/index.cfm**. This is a SJI (State Justice Institute) funded, award winning membership site that serves as a network for practitioners of self-help programs as well as an online clearinghouse of information relating to self representation.

- Legal proceedings can be stressful, so take some time to unwind by experiencing a website called **"The Beauty of Terra"** — Here, peaceful music, relaxing pictures of nature, and inspirational messages combine to diminish whatever stress you may be feeling. Get there by going to the links page of **www.Curryco.cjb.net** (The website that features the publisher of **The Deposition Handbook**) and then clicking on "Tranquil Afternoon."

The number of sites in this chapter doesn't even scratch the surface when it comes to informing you about what legal resources are available on the Internet. If you search for "legal help," you'll quickly discover that hundreds, if not thousands, of legal web sites exist. Narrowing your search to "deposition help" will reduce the number somewhat, but you'll still end up with umpteen choices. So, to keep things manageable, you can start with the resources listed here and then examine a few others you might find helpful or more on target to your specific concerns. And after you've familiarized yourself with some foundational information, it may be time to stop researching and tell yourself, "I understand enough." After that, close the books, turn off the computer, and just know that you'll proceed with confidence in your upcoming deposition.

Much Success!

—oOo—

REFERENCES

Branton, James L., and Jim D. Lovett (1988). California Depositions, Trial Lawyers Series, Volumes I and IA. Ft. Worth, Texas; Knowles Publishing, Inc.

Brown, Peter Megaree, The Art of Questioning: Thirty Maxims of Cross-Examination. (1987). New York: Macmillian Publishing Company.

Crane, Gary M., (1990). Certified Shorthand Reporters Compendium. California and Federal Discovery. Sacramento, California.

Freedman, Joshua; Freedman, Patricia; Jensen, Anabel; and Rideout, Marsha. (1998). Handle With Care: Emotional Intelligence Activity Book, San Mateo, California: Six Seconds.

Goleman, Gary. (1995). Emotional Intelligence: Why It Matters More than IQ (New York). Bantam Dell Publishing.

Johnson (J.D.), Larry G. (1995). The Deposition Guide: A Practical Handbook for Witnesses. Seattle, Washington. (Website: http://www.lulu.com/content/468033)

Related Readings
Bergman, Paul and Berman-Barrett, Sara J., Represent Yourself in Court (1994) Berkeley, California: Nolo Press

Bergman, Paul and Albert J. Moore, Nolo's Deposition Handbook (2005) Berkeley, California: Nolo Press

References Cont'd

Mangiaracina, Michael, <u>Courtroom Testimony Concepts.</u>
(1992). San Clemente, California: Quik-Code Publications.

ABOUT THE AUTHOR

For years, while living in Sacramento, California, Virginia A. Lathan wore two hats: freelance court reporter and freelance writer. One day, she decided she was tired of juggling the demands of both professions, so she had a choice to make: court reporting versus writing. To continue working as a court reporter, she'd make lots of money, but she would have to work long hours doing something that wasn't creative. To work as a writer, she'd have more opportunity to express herself creatively and wouldn't mind working long hours because she loved writing; hence, her work would be her play. Writing won hands down.

Fast forward to 2008.

She now lives in Chicago and writes constantly. "The Deposition Handbook" was her first nonfiction book, and since its publication, she has completed two others: "Preventing Sexual Harassment: A Training Manual for the Workplace," and "Needs Assessment: A Guide for Community Action" (which she co-authored with R. Joanne Guillery). She is currently working on a suspense/thriller novel that she hopes to have in bookstores sometime this year.

Other fiction that she writes are stories to be told. As a member of ASE: Chicago Association of Black Storytellers, she regularly does storytelling performances at such places as schools, libraries, bookstores, and for social groups. To know more about her storytelling ven tures, visit her website at www.GenuinelyGood.cjb. net.

And when she's not writing, she's usually playing tennis and homeschooling her precocious twelve-year old daughter, which is an endeavor that has raised her interest in writing children's books.

INDEX